The PayPal Official Insider Guide to

ONLINE
FUNDRAISING

Raise Money for Your Cause

Jon Ann Lindsey

 **PayPal**™ | Press

DEC   2012

The PayPal Official Insider Guide to Online Fundraising
Jon Ann Lindsey

This PayPal Press book is published by Peachpit.
For information on PayPal Press books, contact:
Peachpit
www.peachpit.com

To report errors, please send a note to errata@peachpit.com

Project Editor: Michael J. Nolan
Development Editor: Jonah Otis
Production Editor: David Van Ness
Copyeditor: Jennifer Needham
Proofreader: Gretchen Dykstra
Indexer: Joy Dean Lee
Cover and Interior Designer: Charlene Charles-Will
Compositor: Myrna Vladic

Notice of Rights

Notice of Liability

The information in this book is distributed on an "As Is" basis without warranty. While every precaution has been taken in the preparation of the book, neither the author nor Peachpit shall have any liability to any person or entity with respect to any loss or damage caused or alleged to be caused directly or indirectly by the instructions contained in this book or by the computer software and hardware products described in it.

While every effort has been made to ensure accuracy at the time of writing, the products and offerings by PayPal, including pricing and the manner in which they are accessed or controlled through www.paypal.com, are subject to change without notice. Subjective statements about the quality of products described in this book are not claims by PayPal but represent the sole opinion of the author.

Trademarks

Many of the designations used by manufacturers and sellers to distinguish their products are claimed as trademarks. Where those designations appear in this book, and Peachpit was aware of a trademark claim, the designations appear as requested by the owner of the trademark. All other product names and services identified throughout this book are used in editorial fashion only and for the benefit of such companies with no intention of infringement of the trademark. No such use, or the use of any trade name, is intended to convey endorsement or other affiliation with this book.

ISBN 13:   978-0-321-83308-2
ISBN 10:   0-321-83308-2

9 8 7 6 5 4 3 2 1

Printed and bound in the United States of America

*For Charley, Judy, Eve, Pam, and future author Tru,
with much love and gratitude for your endless support.*

*And to canine do-gooders Prana and Chi and their
gracious people, Holly and Eric.*

*I'm so fortunate that this project brought me
to your quiet oasis.*

Acknowledgments

Author's Acknowledgments

My sincerest thanks to everyone who helped with the production of this book: PayPal's Matt Jones and Karen Richards for their editing and research; Clam Lorenz and Tanya Urschel for their expertise and advice; Gokul Nair and Marcus Meazzo for their artistic vision; Cynthia Robinson for her legal review; Janet Isadore and Jonah Otis for their support of PayPal Press.

I'm grateful for the guidance of the Peachpit team: Michael Nolan, David Van Ness, and Jennifer Needham, as well as their patience with a newbie author.

The most rewarding part of writing this book was getting to know some of the nonprofit world's respected leaders: Katya Andresen, Alia McKee, Mark Rovner, Sandy Rees, Pat Walsh, Kivi Leroux Miller, Dennis McCarthy, Steve MacLaughlin, and Larry Eason. I benefited so much from your generosity with your ideas, materials, and time, and I know the dedicated people running small nonprofits will benefit even more. Thanks to you all.

PayPal Press Acknowledgments

We applaud PayPal's Nonprofit Engagement Team—Clam Lorenz and Tanya Urschel—whose great subject-matter expertise was matched only by their dedication; Managing Editor Matt Jones, whose expert content strategy assured top editorial quality; Production Editor Karen Richards, whose diligent teamwork mastered our ambitious schedule; and Illustrator Gokul Nair, whose astute artwork enhanced the value of this book.

We'd also like to thank the following PayPal Press executive sponsors for their highly supportive and ongoing creative contributions: Janet Isadore, Jonah Otis, and Marcus Meazzo.

Foreword

If you've ever spent time working for a good cause, you know that fund-raising is an essential part of accomplishing your greater purpose. It doesn't matter if you're taking up a collection for a friend in need, helping a neighbor run for city council, or starting your own 501(c)(3) charity: raising funds effectively can be the difference between mere noble intentions, and realizing a better day for those you're working so hard to help.

For many budding social entrepreneurs, this discovery can be a cause for concern. No matter how committed you are to the cause, asking someone to donate can seem daunting: *What if I'm not good at it? What if they don't like our mission? What if they say no?*

Fortunately, there has never been a better time to be a brand-new fund-raiser. Digital fundraising—using online, mobile, and social tools to raise donations—is the nonprofit sector's fastest-growing channel. Dive in, and you'll find a wide range of ready-to-use digital tools that marry generations of lessons learned with powerful data- and technology-driven solutions. You can go from great idea to dollars collected in just minutes, and you don't need to be a professional to do it.

PayPal is an integral part of that digital fundraising universe. Each year, hundreds of thousands of nonprofits around the world rely on us to process billions of dollars. We power payments for leading fundraising solution providers, and our Donate button is often the starting point for anyone who needs a safe and easy way to collect donations.

PayPal is proud to be trusted by so many good causes. As we define the future of payments, we're mindful that money isn't just used to buy things: it's also a way to address the issues that matter most to us. PayPal is committed to the success of fundraisers, and to the idea that it should be easy for anyone to give to any cause, anytime, anywhere, any way.

—Clam Lorenz
Nonprofit Engagement
PayPal

Contents at a Glance

Contents

Part 3   ONLINE FUNDRAISING MEDIA

Part 4   FUNDRAISING WITH PAYPAL

Introduction

So you have a mission and the passion to reach it. What do you do next?

There are many reasons why people or organizations collect donations, such as

- To help a friend with medical bills

- To support school projects

- To fund research to solve a world problem

- To help a local arts group produce its next show

The needs are almost endless, but there are some commonalities that stretch across most types of fundraising. In the chapters ahead, you will find important insights on what you need to know before you embark on your next campaign. Whether you are an individual, a small organization, or a large nonprofit, we offer many tips on how to gain wider reach and support. We also highlight important industry trends and navigate the new online fundraising technology, which can help you meet your goals.

First, you need to know what kind of people donate and what motivates them. Having a deeper understanding of donor motivations and demographic patterns will help you plan a strategy that yields better results. We give you a tour of the fundraising landscape, which will help you figure out where to put your resources.

Another important aspect of any type of fundraising is to consider the ethical, legal, and tax implications. While this book cannot replace professional guidance, it does provide an overview of these topics to assist you in your planning.

Then there is storytelling. Modern media technology has brought this old tradition to new heights. In this guide, you'll discover how to communicate your mission. There are many simple techniques you can use to make your story resonate with your existing supporters, and to win over new ones. We also point you to solutions that can help you create unique campaigns, as well as track and manage the support you'll gain from them.

Social media, crowdfunding, multichannel—buzzwords everywhere! But what do they really mean? Don't panic. These terms all refer to vehicles that make reaching out to donors more effective. Today, people can connect in more fun, innovative ways than ever before. The "social" topic is crucial, so this guide covers the basics; in addition, we offer a companion book, *The PayPal Official Insider Guide to Social Media*, which examines the topic in more depth.

Mobile, mobile, mobile! If you are on the run like most of us, and need mobile fundraising solutions, jump ahead to Chapter 8, where we share must-haves and new tools like "responsive design," text-to-give, and mobile pledging. After reading this chapter, you will be able to go full speed ahead with a mobile strategy.

Just in the past several years, advances in technology have created tremendous shifts in how we lead our lives. Society is at a pivotal point in time where people are reaching out and engaging with each other in new and exciting ways. At PayPal, we work with many different kinds of customers and partners doing incredible, innovative things with fundraising. We put together this book to share our knowledge. We hope it helps you reach higher ground in your mission.

—Tanya Urschel
PayPal Nonprofit Engagement

Part 1

ONLINE
FUNDRAISING
BASICS

1

Why Online Fundraising?

Are you ready to dip your toe into the online fundraising waters? Are you eager to get going, but concerned that you may be in over your head?

Don't fret—you've come to the right place. We're going to share some simple, effective, and proven ways for beginners to collect money via the Web for good causes.

The first thing we'll do in Chapter 1 is go over some basic principles and processes to give you an overview of the fundraising landscape.

Online Fundraising Defined

Let's take a moment to clarify the term "online fundraising," because it's probably broader than you think.

When you envision online fundraising, you may imagine donors sitting comfortably at their desktop computers and donating through the websites of their favorite charities. And they very well may be.

But it's just as likely that they're connecting to their causes while lolling on the sofa with their iPads, or multitasking with their smartphones or any number of mobile devices.

For simplicity, we'll use "online fundraising" as a catchall that covers raising money through websites, email, social media, or texts, regardless of the type of device used.

Who Do We Think You Are?

We welcome all the readers we can help, of course, but this book will be most useful to those who are new to online fundraising, many of whom are probably new(ish) to offline fundraising, as well.

You're likely to fit into one of these categories:

- Leaders of very small nonprofits, perhaps made up of just yourself and a handful of board members. Paid staff? Probably not yet.

  We figure your budget is tight, so you'll probably want to start with the simplest online solutions, and do more as your organization grows.

  For example, you might just want to be able to accept online donations from your website right now, and then add an email newsletter in your next phase.

- People raising money for existing nonprofits—charities, schools, churches, and the like. PTAs, kids' sports teams, and church youth groups fall into this category.

- People raising money for a nonprofit that's not a charity. Sounds like a trick question, doesn't it? But there are plenty of these organizations—professional associations, labor unions, and veterans' groups, to name a few. The strategies outlined in this book apply to these groups, too.

- People raising money for family, friends, neighbors, or even themselves. There's no nonprofit status involved here, just electronic passing of the hat for someone who needs help, or wants a honeymoon fund, or any number of scenarios.

Fundraising Facts

Traditional offline fundraising takes seemingly countless forms, from humble door-to-door soliciting for a few dollars to swanky charity dinners for $500 a plate.

Online fundraising raises the bar by giving you 24/7 global reach to champion your cause and request money. Each approach offers variations on the same pitch: asking people to give funds to benefit something other than themselves.

Even in tough economic times, people often respond to these requests with open wallets. While corporate and foundation grants provide significant funding for some nonprofit organizations, the vast majority comes from just plain folks giving to causes they believe in. In 2011, individuals donated 73 percent of the $298.4 billion given to nonprofits in the U.S. (**Figure 1.1**). Further, about 65 percent of American households gave to at least one nonprofit organization during the year.

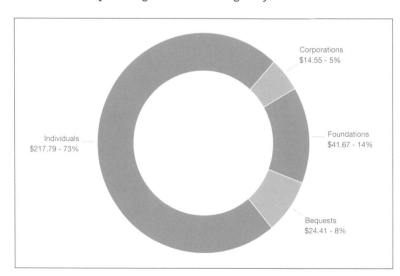

Corporations
$14.55 - 5%

Foundations
$41.67 - 14%

Individuals
$217.79 - 73%

Bequests
$24.41 - 8%

Figure 1.1

Individuals gave almost $218 billion to nonprofits in 2011, more than the other major sources combined.

Source: Giving USA Foundation

Who did all that money go to? Of the roughly $218 billion that individuals donated to nonprofits in 2011, fully 32 percent went to religious organizations, followed by educational institutions with 13 percent, and human services groups with 12 percent (**Figure 1.2**).

Figure 1.2

Religious organizations topped all group recipients in 2011.

Source: Giving USA Foundation

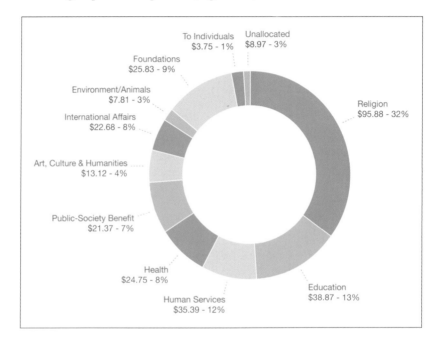

These statistics may help you appreciate the scope of fundraising at a high level. But what do they mean for your cause? Who will your donors be, and how should you appeal to them?

Read on: Our upcoming chapters will address the issues you're likely to encounter and offer some strategies for online fundraising success.

Types of Online Fundraising

Our book's focus is on fundraising by very small nonprofits and individuals. Think of it as the do-it-yourself approach, as opposed to the sophisticated fundraising operations of established nonprofits and very large charities such as the Red Cross or the World Food Program.

While nonprofits of any size share the same goal of raising money for their programs and operations, small organizations and individual fundraisers face a different set of challenges.

Unlike established nonprofits, many up-and-comers simply don't know how to begin the process of online fundraising: how to set up a website, how to appeal to donors, how to collect and distribute funds, how to track contacts, and so on.

We'll help with these concerns and more, keeping in mind that you're probably tight on both money and staffing.

PayPal INSIDER

 ## More Donation Options with PayPal Here™

In 2011, PayPal processed more than $3 billion in donations for some 200,000 nonprofits through its online Donate button, and billions more through various PayPal merchant payment tools.

Now the launch of PayPal Here in 2012 provides a mobile payment solution (photo) that includes a free mobile app and a thumb-sized card reader that plugs into your smartphone.

The new PayPal Here service allows nonprofits to accept in-person donations or payments simply by using a smartphone for transactions. Now donors have the immediate opportunity and nonprofits have the added flexibility to transact money for auction items, team T-shirts, sponsorships, and more *on the spot* at charity events with credit cards, checks (U.S. only), cash, and/or PayPal

balances through the security and convenience of their PayPal account.

For more information, go to www.PayPal.com/here.

PayPal Here in use.

Who's Who in Online Fundraising

Let's take a moment here to look at who participates in online fundraising (**Figure 1.3**). The Asker and Giver roles are obvious, but they're not the only participants involved, especially when you take into account the many resources that can make those roles easier:

- **Fundraiser:** The person or organization requesting a donation.

- **Donor:** The person being asked.

- **Beneficiary:** The person who ends up with the money. It could be your friend who has cancer, a charity, a political candidate, a school, a church, a neighborhood group, a fraternal club, or any individual or organization.

- **Enablers:** The entire industry of experts, researchers, technology providers, and others who can help you raise funds.

PayPal INSIDER

 ## Kiva: Facilitating Person-to-Person Microloans

In Swahili, "Kiva" means "unity" or "agreement." In the world of microfinance, it has come to mean a global community of people connected through lending.

Matt and Jessica Flannery were in their 20s and married only a few months when they began to understand the power of microfinance to improve the lives of the working poor in developing countries. For the next year, they struggled to find out how to make a microloan to a specific entrepreneur in a particular country.

Finally, they decided to just begin. In April 2005, seven businesses were funded through the newly established Kiva.org, with loans totaling $3,500.

Six months later, every loan had been repaid.

Kiva has since grown into one of the world's largest microfinance facilitators. It aggregates small amounts of money—from just $25—to make loans around the world.

Kiva's lending platform has used PayPal as its exclusive processor of online payments.

"PayPal gives us the ability to do something quite remarkable—combine millions of small transactions to fund millions of dollars worth of small business loans to the working poor in the developing world," says Fiona Ramsey, Kiva's public relations director.

"There's something special about choosing an entrepreneur, making a $25 loan, clicking Send, and knowing that person is going to receive your $25 contribution on the other side of the world," she says.

For more information, go to www.Kiva.org.

You'll get to know these participants in this book and in your online inter-actions. Many will introduce themselves to you at the most opportune times in your fundraising efforts. Some may even be *you* as your online fundraising experiences, ambitions, abilities, and achievements grow.

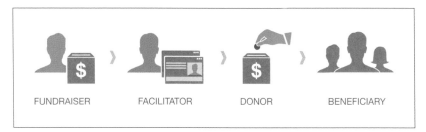

FUNDRAISER   FACILITATOR   DONOR   BENEFICIARY

Figure 1.3 *There are at least four main roles—and many variations—that people can play in the online fundrais-ing process—and you need to know each of them well to succeed.*

The Online Fundraising Cycle

Individual fundraisers and many small nonprofit organizations typi-cally don't need overly complicated documents outlining their fundrais-ing purposes and strategy (unless they're required for legal reasons), but familiarizing yourself with the online fundraising cycle (**Figure 1.4**) will help guide your actions.

There are always some variations to suit specific causes, of course, but the following five steps offer surefire procedures for most of your basic online fundraising needs.

Planning

Online fundraising allows you to be fast and flexible, but you still need a thorough, well-thought-out plan. Begin by asking yourself the following questions: How much money do I need? How will I use it? Where will I get it? What steps will that entail for me? See Chapter 5 for a sample case statement.

When your plan takes shape, remember to view it from the online donors' perspective as well: imagine explaining your fundraising needs to them and making a pitch about why your cause deserves their support. Always be clear, concise, and motivating about your needs, online or off.

Figure 1.4 *The online fundraising cycle involves Internet synergy that helps keep donations moving in your direction.*

Prospecting

In the early stages of a fundraising campaign, you'll want to identify potential online donors and learn more about current supporters as well. This could involve Internet research, or scouring Twitter and Facebook for people who are interested in causes like yours.

Most likely, new supporters will find you through already established online relationships, such as your own contacts or friends of your current donors.

We'll have more to say on this subject in upcoming chapters, about donor behavior (Chapter 3) and social fundraising (Chapter 9).

Cultivation

Communicating with current and prospective donors is part of the careful cultivation you'll need to do to keep online money coming in for your cause. This can include sending e-newsletters and website updates, tweeting your latest happenings, keeping your Facebook page up to date, sharing real-time and/or podcast presentations, or even hosting online forums.

When you've identified prospective donors, keep in touch, provide them with updated information about your cause and its accomplishments, and be sure to thank them for their interest.

Solicitation

Now there's a word that can make your palms sweat. However laudable a cause, asking for money can be tricky. Luckily, there are a number of smart ways to do it.

Blogs, webpages, emails, social media, and online events can help you ask for donations in broad and sustainable ways.

We'll share more about the where, why, when, and how of effective online solicitation throughout this book (especially in Chapter 3, where we explain key aspects of online donor behavior).

Stewardship

This step in the cycle involves effectively managing your relationship with donors. Managing money responsibly builds the trust you need to turn one-time donors into repeat donors. As your relationship deepens, your supporters are more likely to tell others about your good works and help grow your base.

Another huge part of stewardship is making sure your supporters know how much you appreciate them. Inattentive fundraisers eventually find that some donors stop giving because they don't feel adequately thanked. Savvy fundraisers know how to treat donors as well as their donations.

Helping Hand

With this overview, we trust that you have a general sense of online fundraising and are ready for more insights and applications.

Here are some points to remember as you read on:

- Online fundraising refers to raising money on your website or mobile app or other digital media (that is, finding money for your cause on whatever platforms serve you best).

- Individuals raise billions of dollars a year for nonprofits such as churches, schools, and charities.

- You don't have to be a nonprofit to accept donations. Individuals can readily raise money for causes that support sick friends or relatives, pay unexpected bills, or serve other urgent needs.

In Chapter 2, we'll look at specific online fundraising techniques and share some quick ways to get set up and start collecting money for your cause.

2

Think Outside
the Envelope

Whether your fundraising goal is $500 or $50,000, your coffers will fill faster if supporters can donate online or by mobile phone.

Many organizations and individuals use their online presence merely to provide information about themselves, like an electronic brochure. But those that take the next step—actively using the Web to fundraise—are tapping into the fastest-growing platform for bringing in money.

Getting started is easier than you might think, even for shoestring operations and people who aren't tech-savvy.

Let's look at some of the reasons donors, individuals, and nonprofits are embracing online and mobile fundraising.

Clicking on the Rise

Schools, churches, arts groups, health organizations—they all rely on donations to help fund their missions. Neighbors rally to raise money for fire victims or to restore local landmarks, and we all know someone who's helped an ailing friend or relative by taking up a collection.

About 90 percent of donations are still made face-to-face or through the old-school check in the mail. But overall, direct mail is becoming less popular as a fundraising method, and online giving is increasing. In the years ahead, online donations will continue to gain share from direct mail, and will grow even further as the 33 percent of nonprofits that don't yet fundraise online take that step.

It's really no wonder that donors increasingly prefer the keyboard or the mobile phone to the check and the envelope. Convio, an Austin, Texas–based company that makes software for nonprofits, conducted a survey in 2008 of 3,400 "wired wealthy" donors—those who reported giving almost $11,000 a year on average.

Although 80 percent were "multichannel" donors, meaning they gave both online and by mail, 51 percent said they preferred online giving. About 30 percent preferred giving by mail.

The following statements about the benefits of online giving received the greatest support (strongly agree or somewhat agree) among survey participants:

- Online giving is more efficient and helps charities reduce their administrative expenses (72 percent).

- Online giving lets you make a gift immediately when you're thinking about it, where otherwise you might forget (70 percent).

- Online giving lets charities respond more quickly in the event of a crisis or emergency (68 percent).

Garnering less support but still worth noting were two other considerations:

- Using credit cards to donate online gives frequent flyer miles or other rewards (53 percent).

- Online giving makes it easier to track donations over time (48 percent).

Causes We Care About

The most common fundraising scenario involves individuals giving their time, effort, and dollars to causes that affect their daily lives. If you've ever collected money for your children's soccer team or for computers for their school, you know what it's like to make a difference.

You also have plenty of company: PayPal research shows that 15 percent of adults in the United States fundraise at least once a year, raising an average of $400 each time they take up a cause.

Individual Fundraising

The top reasons individuals fundraise (**Figure 2.1**) include the following:

1. **Education:** No surprise here. Think of how many parents tirelessly raise money for schools (gift wrap, anyone?) to help with supplies, band instruments, field trips, infrastructure, or any number of other needs.

2. **Health/illness:** When a friend or relative falls ill, no gift is more practical than some extra money to cover medical bills or household expenses.

3. **Basic needs:** People like to make their community a better place, and many make their contribution by helping to provide food and shelter for the needy.

Interestingly, the type of institution for which individuals most often fundraise is schools, but the top institutions to which people give money are religious organizations. The likely explanation is that most people don't fundraise on behalf of their church, they just donate to it directly.

From a process standpoint, individual fundraising is completely straight-forward: you do all the work! You ask for and collect the money, and then manage its distribution by buying the needed items or giving the cash to the coach or school or other recipients.

Figure 2.1

Individual fundraising is heavily weighted toward education and health-related causes.

Source: PayPal, Ipsos Omnibus Online

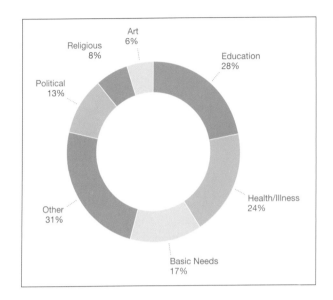

NONPROFIT SUCCESS STORY

 Through the Eyes of Elise

Andy and Heather Steingruebl's foray into online and offline fundraising started shortly after their daughter Elise was diagnosed with leukemia in 2010 at the age of six.

In the dark days after the diagnosis, Heather says that what kept them going was the knowledge that Elise had a very good chance of survival, thanks in large part to the work of the Leukemia & Lymphoma Society (LLS).

"Survival rates across all blood cancers have doubled and tripled in the last 20 years," Heather says. And the survival rate for childhood leukemia has increased from just 4 percent to over 85 percent today. Thanks in part to donor-funded research sponsored by LLS, we get to be part of this very hopeful statistic, too."

Elise has been active in fundraising, too, joining her mom and dad—a PayPal employee—to support the Silicon Valley chapter of LLS.

A Facebook page called "Through the Eyes of Elise" promoted a series of videos the intrepid junior reporter posted to YouTube, in which she interviewed cancer researchers, LLS staffers, and her hero, San Jose Sharks hockey player Patrick Marleau, to increase awareness and raise money to help fight leukemia.

See her videos at www.youtube.com/user/EyesofElise.

Elise Steingruebl's YouTube interviews have helped raise money to fight childhood leukemia.

Fundraising for Nonprofits

Another type of fundraising occurs when individuals raise money on behalf of a nonprofit—think of the familiar Team in Training walks for the Leukemia & Lymphoma Society or the Relay for Life for the American Cancer Society. In this scenario, participants solicit donations from their friends and coworkers and turn the money over to the sponsoring charity.

Whether people are raising money on their own or for an organization, there's a whole lot of asking going on. Imagine how many calls, letters, and emails have been exchanged to bring the Relay for Life's total income to more than $4 billion since its inception in 1985.

The numbers prove that people are willing to ask for donations for causes they believe in, but that doesn't mean they're entirely comfortable doing so, or that they wouldn't appreciate tools to make it easier.

All but the most natural salespeople have probably run up against some of fundraising's common barriers:

1. **Getting started:** How do you set a goal? Whom do you contact? (And, perhaps, why did you get yourself into this?)

2. **Fear of soliciting:** It's awkward to ask for money. No one wants to imagine he's the guy with the donation cup in front of the neighborhood grocery store, watching his friends flee across the parking lot.

3. **Money handling:** The more you raise, the more work you make for yourself. It's no fun dealing with cash and all those checks (fingers crossed that they clear) and all those trips to the bank.

4. **Managing contacts:** Keeping track of donors, updating them on your progress, and sending thank-you notes can seem like daunting obligations.

Online donation tools can relieve some of that pain as surely as ibuprofen after a three-day charity walk. At the most basic level, you can request money by sending your contacts an email or a text with a link to a donation page, or by cutting and pasting a Donate button into a website or blog. And there are plenty of resources to help with planning and goal setting. We'll talk about these later in this book.

TIP: Stagger your programs—don't overload friends and family with donation requests. Stick to only a few fundraising programs a year, and target requests to specific donor interests.

Nearly every nonprofit these days has at least a website and a Facebook page. Given their broad reach, turning these into fundraising channels is job one for many organizations.

According to Toronto-based Artez Interactive, a provider of online fundraising tools, online donors tend to be younger and more affluent than offline donors, and they give more. The average online donation has consistently increased, doubling over the past four years.

Furthermore, online giving is particularly cost-effective for charities. While it can cost $1 to $1.25 to acquire a new donor through direct mail and more than 63 cents through telemarketing, the cost per dollar of raising money online can be as little as 5 cents.

Sources: *Fund-Raising Cost Effectiveness*, by James Greenfield; *Cost-Effectiveness of Nonprofit Telemarketing Campaigns*, by Keating, Parsons and Roberts; and Network for Good.

BY THE NUMBERS

 ## Largest U.S. Charities

These organizations topped *Forbes* magazine's list of the biggest public charities for 2011, based on the private donations they received:

Charity	Private Support (in millions)
United Way	$3,859
Salvation Army	$1,807
Feeding America	$1,145
American National Red Cross	$1,077
Food for the Poor	$1,037
American Cancer Society	$903
AmeriCares Foundation	$794
Catholic Charities USA	$794
World Vision	$779
YMCA	$767

A Toolkit for Giving and Receiving

The trend toward online and mobile fundraising is undeniable. When you're asking for money, you surely want to make it as easy as possible for people to say yes. And let's face it, sometimes even the hassle of finding the checkbook and a stamp can spell the death of a donation.

But for individual fundraisers and small nonprofits, going digital can feel intimidating, too. Sure, you want donating to be effortless for givers, but what about the effort on your part? Nonprofits are well known for running lean operations and relying on volunteers. They may not have a lot of time or skill for setting up and maintaining a regular website, much less one that involves financial transactions.

Luckily, the effort isn't exhaustive. PayPal and other companies provide a range of tools that can have you collecting donations as quickly as you can cut and paste. We'll suggest a few PayPal solutions here, and you can find more details throughout this book.

Just remember, new technology becomes available all the time, and the players sometimes come and go, so it's always worthwhile to do some research on the most current offerings.

If you or your group has a PayPal Premier or Business account, you're ready to get started. If not, you can go to www.paypal.com to sign up.

TIP: For complete information on fundraising with PayPal, individuals can go to www.paypal.com/fundraising. Nonprofits can go to www.paypal.com/nonprofit.

The PayPal Donate Button

Probably the easiest and fastest way to accept donations through PayPal on a website is to add a Donate button. You don't have to worry about code: PayPal provides the HTML, which you can copy and paste to create a button (**Figure 2.2**) or a link to put in an email.

Donors click the button or link and donate with a credit card, debit card, or PayPal account. All donations go directly into your group's PayPal account for easy tracking.

There are no setup or monthly fees, just transaction fees based on how much you receive and whether you're a registered nonprofit.

Figure 2.2 *Donors click the Donate button or link and choose whether to pay by credit card, debit card, or PayPal account.*

TIP: To receive discounted rates, sign up for a PayPal Business account. Select Nonprofit as the business type, and Charity as the category.

To confirm your nonprofit status, log in to your PayPal account one day after initial signup and submit the following items through the Resolution Center:

- Evidence of tax-exempt status
- Bank statement or voided check in your organization's name
- PayPal email account
- Contact information
- Description of your organization and type of payments you want to accept (such as donations or merchandise payments)

The PayPal Request Money Tool

Use the PayPal Request Money tool to solicit donations from your friends and family by email, mobile phone, or the Web (**Figure 2.3**).

You fill out the request information, then an email alerts your potential donors to log in and make a payment using their PayPal balance, bank transfer, or credit card. To give, donors transfer funds from their PayPal account into yours. If they don't have a PayPal account, they can sign up when they receive your alert.

Figure 2.3 *The Request Money tool sends potential donors an email. They can use their PayPal balance, bank transfer, or credit card to donate.*

The PayPal Giving Widget

You can also make donating to your cause easier by placing a custom PayPal Giving Widget on your website or blog. You can:

- Post your widget to your website or blog in just a few clicks.

- Acknowledge top contributors to your cause.

- Process contributions simply.

Go to http://giving.paypallabs.com to get started.

Facebook App by FundRazr

PayPal and FundRazr have worked together on a crowdfunding app to raise money and awareness for your causes, and convert your donors into advocates.

You can share your FundRazr campaign through Facebook, Twitter, email, your blog, and your website. Causes you can fund include:

- **Personal causes:** Medical, travel, or education costs, personal losses, family tragedies, support for a friend, memorials, pet healthcare

- **Group causes:** Sports teams, school groups, community groups, churches, arts groups, animal shelters, school reunions

- **Political campaigns:** Campaigns at the local, state, or federal level

- **Nonprofits and charities:** Registered charities at the local, state, federal, or international level

Go to http://fundrazr.com/paypal-social for more information.

Other PayPal Partner Tools

- Convio, a Blackbaud company, is the leading provider of on-demand constituent engagement solutions for nonprofits.

- DonateNow from Network for Good offers branded donation pages, reports, and other services for online fundraising.

- StayClassy is a leading provider of fundraising management software for nonprofit organizations.

- Artez Interactive provides friendship-powered mobile, social, and online fundraising solutions.

PROGRESS BENCHMARKS

 Small Nonprofit Growth

Online giving is growing fastest for small organizations, according to a 2011 Benchmark Report by Convio. In fact, organizations with fewer than 10,000 email addresses saw a 26 percent increase in online giving.

How does your organization compare? If you run a healthcare nonprofit, your growth is among the most prolific. The Convio study notes that healthcare nonprofits with mailing lists numbering as few as 5,000 addresses were the most successful in attracting new donors.

- Give.mobi provides a cost-effective way for nonprofits to accept donations from smartphone users.

- Pay It Square collects money from people online for events, fundraisers, or other types of group payments.

- GoFundMe offers easy online fundraising with simple personal donation websites.

Helping Hand

Are you ready to branch out with your fundraising efforts? Good! Here are some key points to keep in mind:

- Online is the fastest-growing fundraising channel for nonprofits.

- Individuals, fledgling organizations, and established enterprises alike can raise money online.

- If you can email, you can fundraise. You don't need technical skills to get started.

Next, in Chapter 3, we'll discuss donor behavior and how it can inform your fundraising tactics.

3

What Makes Donors Click

A fortunate few nonprofits have the luxury of conducting market research to glean insights about their donors, or to test various fundraising approaches to see which work best. In scrappier organizations, donation requests might be produced by the same person who answers the phone, wrangles volunteers, and takes the trash out.

It may take more effort for smaller groups to zero in on what motivates their supporters to click the Donate button, but leaders in the nonprofit sector have plenty of tips to minimize guesswork.

Read on for some of their best practices.

Why People Give— Science Has Its Say

Why do people give to charity, anyway? Or give to their alma mater, or their professional association, or an unemployed acquaintance whose puppy got hit by a car?

There are lots of reasons, from quite lofty to stunningly simple. First up: lofty. According to nonprofit experts Katya Andresen, Alia McKee, and Mark Rovner (see sidebar), biology has encouraging news for the fundraisers of the world:

- Humans are genetically hardwired to help each other. It seems that goodness is an adaptive trait that has helped us survive as a species. (See? Lofty.)

- People are also wired for empathy. When we see images or hear stories about other people's plights, we experience them as if they were our own, and we want to make things better.

- When we act on these impulses, we activate the pleasure centers of our brain. Giving makes us feel good!

Here's more donor behavior insight from Andresen, McKee, and Rovner:

- Emotions prevail when it comes to motivating people to give to causes. Example: One of McKee's nonprofit clients started a program to call a wide group of donors to thank them personally for their support.

  Half of the donors got a gracious call from a staff member in the organization. The other half received calls from Bhutanese refugees who had resettled in the United States with the organization's help.

  Not surprisingly, repeat donations within two months of the calls were three to four times higher from the group that got a call from a refugee. Further, refugees who told their tales with more emotion generated higher donations than those who were more matter-of-fact.

- Big numbers are numbing. In a rational world, you'd think we'd want to help as many people as possible. But studies consistently show that givers are most responsive when they identify with a single person in need. When a problem seems too big, people feel like nothing they do will make a difference.

- People follow authority. Really, when's the last time you even saw a "Question Authority" bumper sticker? Much more typical is that people are surprisingly obedient.

  In one oft-recalled experiment, a researcher crossed a street against the signal light while dressed in a business suit and tie, and then again wearing casual clothes. When he wore the suit—dressed as the boss, you might say—3.5 times as many bystanders blithely (and illegally) followed him across the street as when he was dressed as a worker bee.

- Peer pressure works, at any age. Finally, mom gets her answer: Yes, we probably would jump off a cliff if our friends told us to. We're easily persuaded by people we like. That's why Tupperware sales doubled back in the day when friends started selling the burping bowls to other friends.

Industry INSIDER

 ### Meet Three Online Fundraising Experts

Katya Andresen, chief strategy officer of Network for Good, and Alia McKee and Mark Rovner, of the consulting firm Sea Change Strategies, have delved deeply into the science of giving.

Their study of behavioral economics—the social, cognitive, and emotional factors that go into decision making—formed the basis of their two popular e-books on the subject.

The e-books are titled *Homer Simpson for Nonprofits: The Truth About How People Really Think & What It Means for Promoting Your Cause,*

Alia McKee   Mark Rovner   Katya Andresen

and *Lisa Simpson for Nonprofits: What Science Can Teach You About Fundraising, Marketing and Making Social Change.*

They're available as free downloads at www.fundraising123.org.

So, if people are generous all the way down to their genes, it almost makes you wonder why they aren't giving money to your cause every day.

Andresen and her colleagues looked into that question too, and they found that empathy alone isn't enough to unlock our innate generosity. For that, you have to understand how people think and why they act.

And guess what: people tend to be a little irrational, but in a fairly predictable way. Research shows time and again that people donate based on feelings more than thinking—so you want to appeal more to the heart than the head.

When people think more, they give less.

Here's another example. Recently, a trendy hotel chain that wanted to "greenify" its image tested a few messages to encourage guests to reuse their towels. The most effective one didn't even mention conserving water or taking it easy on overtaxed Mother Earth. It simply said, "A majority of guests in this room reuse their towels. Will you join them?" Many did. When made aware of what other people were doing, 33 percent more guests complied.

Behavioral economics is fascinating stuff, isn't it? But your task as a fundraiser isn't to probe the nooks and crannies of your supporters' brains. You just want them to buy some blankets for the homeless or contribute enough money to keep the library open a few more hours a week.

PROGRESS BENCHMARKS

 ### Heart over Head

The following anecdote from *Lisa Simpson for Nonprofits*, by Katya Andresen, Alia McKee, and Mark Rovner, illustrates how rationality can be trumped by emotion when donors consider the value of giving.

Researcher Christopher Olivola has studied charity endurance events like walk-a-thons. The bigger the effort by participants, the more money raised. And the more pain participants experienced, the more their friends were likely to give in support.

Further research showed just how important this spirit of sacrifice can be. People were asked to react to two different ethical scenarios. First, there was a doctor who ran a successful practice in Hollywood, earning $700,000 per year and giving $20,000 to Doctors Without Borders to save 500 lives. Second, there was a different doctor, who actually worked for Doctors Without Borders in developing countries and made $18,000 per year and saved 200 lives.

Which job choice was better? The second, lower-paid doctor, even though he saved fewer lives, said the research subjects. No doubt about it, the heart—and sacrifice—mattered most.

For that, let's take those scientific principles and apply them to everyday life. Here are some key donor communication ideas from the pros:

Avoid numbers for their own sake. Limit statistics and numbers in your communications. Focus on one motivating number—more than that is too much.

Don't convey the complexity of issues. Avoid showing shades of gray. Think black and white.

Show people in need. Share the faces and tell the dramatic stories of the people affected by your cause.

Highlight individuals. Instead of a success story on your website that says, "More than 1,000 children in the county receive food for the weekend through our program," try, "Third-grader Isabella didn't always have enough to eat on weekends when her free school lunch wasn't available. But now she takes home a bag of fresh fruit, cereal, and pasta every Friday."

Have constituents do outreach on your behalf. Track their willingness to serve as spokespeople for your cause.

Show your progress. Put a meter on your website to track your fundraising goal. When people see that others are participating in your campaign, they're more inclined to join.

Show authorities in action. Give your CEO and prominent staffers a personal voice in your communications. Groom some authoritative spokespeople within your organization.

Give contributors something to do. Once you win people over, tell them what you want them to do. Do you want them to take an action? Make a donation? Be specific so you don't squander an opportunity.

Why People Give—the People Themselves Weigh In

We've touched on some of the high-level reasons why people give to charity. There are plenty of nuts-and-bolts reasons, too. For example, if you think people donate because they care deeply about this cause or that, you're mostly right. But that's not the main motivator.

The most common reason people give to a cause is that someone asked them to. It doesn't get much simpler than that.

Convio, a software maker for nonprofits, says friend-to-friend communication is an important element of fundraising strategy. In the company's 2010 study, *The Next Generation of American Giving,* 52 percent of all donors ranked "friends asking for money" as a very appropriate channel to receive a charitable solicitation, outpacing printed mail (41 percent) and email from a charity (28 percent).

 TIP: Invite more (and larger) donations on your website by suggesting an amount. It's easier for visitors to click a $10, $25, or $50 donation button than to wonder how much money is appropriate. Choose the suggestions carefully, knowing that given a choice of low, middle, and high amounts, most donors will go with the middle number.

Lesson? Ask for donations! More important lesson? Ask for more than just donations. Make the most of peer power by asking your supporters to spread the word about your cause through their social networks, and have them ask their friends to do the same.

Industry INSIDER

Why People Give

Network for Good has identified 15 reasons why people donate. When you start a new fundraising campaign, take some time to review the list and make sure that your request taps into at least a few, including:

1. Someone I know asked me to give, and I wanted to help.

2. I felt emotionally moved by someone's story.

3. I want to feel I'm not powerless and can help others (especially during disasters).

4. I want to feel I'm changing someone's life.

5. I feel a sense of closeness to a community or group.

6. I need a tax deduction.

7. I want to memorialize someone struggling with chronic illness or who died of a disease.

8. I was raised to give to charity.

9. Supporting this charity (e.g., wearing its wristband) is in style.

10. Giving makes me feel connected to other people and builds my social network.

11. I want to have a good image of myself/my company.

12. I want to leave a legacy that perpetuates me, my ideals, or my cause.

13. I feel fortunate (or guilty) and want to give something back to others.

14. I give for religious reasons.

15. I want to be seen as a leader/role model.

Givers Give in Many Ways

Even if your nonprofit consists of you and a few board members, or if you're just a well-intentioned individual who isn't part of a nonprofit, you can reap the benefits of online fundraising.

Blackbaud, a maker of nonprofit fundraising software, crunches the data of almost 2,000 nonprofits every year for its *Online Giving Report*. Company researchers found that online giving grew 13 percent in 2011 over 2010 (**Figures 3.1** and **3.2**). Direct mail, by contrast, has been on the decline since 2005.

Online Giving Growth by Organization Size	
Size	Year-Over-Year Change
Small (Less than $1M)	12.8%
Medium ($1M–$10M)	13.1%
Large ($10M+)	8.6%
Total	13.1%

Excluding large international affairs organizations

Figure 3.1 *Online giving grew in all size categories from 2010 to 2011. Blackbaud excluded large international affairs organizations because the data was skewed by the extraordinary giving to Haiti in 2010.*

Source: Blackbaud, *The 2011 Online Giving Report*

Percentage of Total Online Fundraising by Size	
Size	% of Total
Small (Less than $1M)	15.3%
Medium ($1M–$10M)	40.2%
Large ($10M+)	44.5%
Total	100.0%

Figure 3.2 *Small- and medium-size nonprofits made up more than half of all online giving in 2011.*

Source: Blackbaud

Nevertheless, it's still too soon to toss out all your stamps and declare yourself a paperless operation. The fact is, the majority of donors still give by mail, and an increasing number give both offline and online— so-called "multichannel" donors.

Donors' preferences about how they like to give and how they like to be contacted depend on demographics. If your organization has established donors and your mailings already get a great response, you could be on a solid path for years to come. But if one of your goals is to appeal to a younger group, there's a good chance that your literature will go straight from the mailbox to the recycling bin unseen.

Convio looked at the differences in giving habits of four generations in the United States in its 2010 study, *The Next Generation of American Giving:*

Matures

- Born 1945 or earlier

- Population: 39 million

- Estimated 79 percent give to charity

Boomers

- Born 1946 to 1964

- Population: 78 million

- Estimated 67 percent give to charity

Gen X

- Born 1965 to 1980

- Population: 62 million

- Estimated 58 percent give to charity

Gen Y

- Born 1981 to 1991

- Population: 51 million

- Estimated 56 percent give to charity

The age groups that give the most—Baby Boomers and Matures—do so most often by mail. In contrast, only about a quarter of Gen Y donors give by mail (**Figure 3.3**).

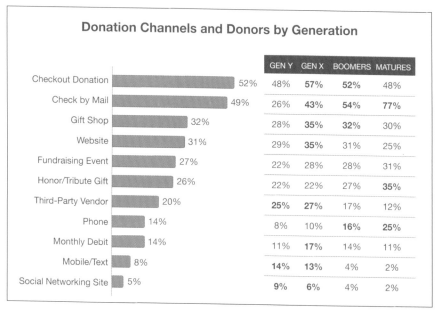

Donation Channels and Donors by Generation		GEN Y	GEN X	BOOMERS	MATURES
Checkout Donation	52%	48%	57%	52%	48%
Check by Mail	49%	26%	43%	54%	77%
Gift Shop	32%	28%	35%	32%	30%
Website	31%	29%	35%	31%	25%
Fundraising Event	27%	22%	28%	28%	31%
Honor/Tribute Gift	26%	22%	22%	27%	35%
Third-Party Vendor	20%	25%	27%	17%	12%
Phone	14%	8%	10%	16%	25%
Monthly Debit	14%	11%	17%	14%	11%
Mobile/Text	8%	14%	13%	4%	2%
Social Networking Site	5%	9%	6%	4%	2%

Figure 3.3 *At left are the various channels donors used from 2008 to 2010. At right is the percentage of people who used each channel. Giving through a website increases with younger populations, culminating in Gen Y, which gives more online than by mail. Blue percentages represent a statistically significant difference.*

Credit: Convio, *The Next Generation of American Giving*, 2010

Baby Boomers, Gen X, and Gen Y give through various channels, including e-commerce, online, event fundraising, tributes, monthly debit programs, and mobile/text donations. Furthermore, the younger the donor, the more likely they are to give in multiple ways.

Focus groups with Gen X and Gen Y also found that these people are "channel-hoppers" in making donations to causes in multiple ways: they might text money in an emergency, write a check at an event, and share a credit card with a telemarketer.

The Most Wonderful Time of the Year

It could be the spirit of giving, or it could be the spirit of getting a tax deduction before the year's over, but most online giving happens in December (**Figure 3.4**).

Many donors give to their favorite causes at the end of the year out of habit or in response to special holiday campaigns. Blackbaud's Steve MacLaughlin, however, cautions against putting so much emphasis on year-end giving that you neglect other times of the year, figuring you'll catch up in December.

TIP: One way to get your end-of-year email noticed is to craft a grabby subject line. "Last chance" and "tax deduction?" Ho (ho ho) hum. But the intrigue of "73,000,003 reasons" makes you want to open the email to find out more.

MacLaughlin, who blogs about nonprofit research and trends at npEngage, www.npengage.com, says donors' email inboxes are flooded with requests during the holidays, so it's difficult to stand out if you don't already have a relationship with someone.

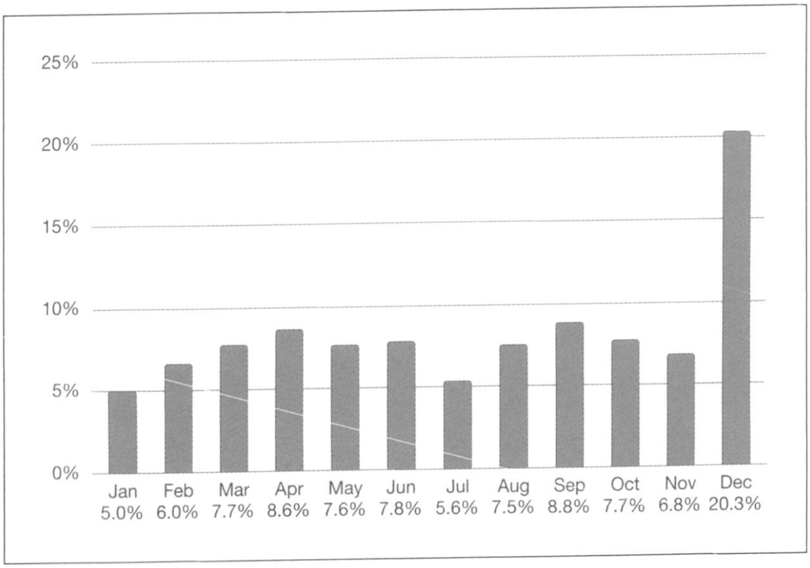

Figure 3.4

End-of-year giving continues to account for most online donations. 34.8 percent of online giving in 2011 happened in October, November, and December.

Source: Blackbaud

	Jan	Feb	Mar	Apr	May	Jun	Jul	Aug	Sep	Oct	Nov	Dec
	5.0%	6.0%	7.7%	8.6%	7.6%	7.8%	5.6%	7.5%	8.8%	7.7%	6.8%	20.3%

He recommends that nonprofits set incremental fundraising goals focused on other times of the year. A lot of money flows to higher education in June, for example, as part of universities' end-of-fiscal-year drives. In health care, April and September are popular months for events, taking the pressure off the final months of the year.

Helping Hand

In this chapter, we learned some fundamentals of donor behavior that apply both online and off, including:

- The most effective pitches appeal to people's emotions.

- People are strongly influenced by peers, so ask your supporters to enlist their friends.

- Take a multichannel approach to communications. Different demographic groups have different preferences.

4

A Wealth of Fundraising Options

The innovators in online fundraising are an ambitious lot, always introducing new tools and websites to help nonprofits achieve their goals. They're so good at it that you might think you're leaving money on the table if you don't pursue every avenue that pops up. But that's not practical. One way to set priorities is to consider who or what you're raising money for (a person? sports team? charity?) and choose the websites and services that fit your scenario. We'll go through some of those options here.

Getting to Know the Online Neighborhoods

There are dozens, if not hundreds, of websites that cater to U.S. fundraisers by processing payments and perhaps providing research and advice, event planning resources, and marketing assistance. Many of them process donations only for registered 501(c)(3) organizations—the schools, churches, and welfare nonprofits that come to mind when we think of tax-exempt charities.

Other giving websites have no such restrictions, and make it dead simple to raise money not only for charities and people in need, but also for weddings, vacations, tattoos, removal of tattoos, and anything else people hit up their friends to pay for.

Nonprofits and individuals can establish or expand their online presence in a number of ways. These categories aren't neat and tidy, and some of the terminology is still in flux, but here's a rough breakdown of the online venues where nonprofits can set up shop:

- Their own website, where supporters can give through donation pages and buttons.

- Social giving websites such as FundRazr, Indiegogo, Crowdrise, and GoFundMe, also called peer-to-peer or crowdfunding sites. Nonprofits can set up campaigns on these websites, but the emphasis for some is on empowering the individual fundraiser. Anyone can quickly create a page for a cause and use social media to invite friends to contribute. (We'll take an in-depth look at social fundraising in Chapter 9.)

- Charity portals, such as Charity Navigator and GuideStar, which list and evaluate thousands of public charities. Visitors can research organizations and donate through the portals.

- Facebook, Twitter, LinkedIn, and other social media websites. This is where fundraising is getting interesting and experimental, if not reliably lucrative (yet). Organizations can set up their own Facebook page and Twitter account to communicate with supporters—nothing new there—and their supporters can add apps and widgets (Causes, FundRazr) to their personal pages on behalf of their favorite charities.

In another twist, HelpAttack! lets social media lovers pledge a small amount to a charity each time they tweet or update their Facebook status, or add a pin on Pinterest.

Success Begins at Home

Whew! There's a lot to "Like" out there, as they say on Facebook. But keeping a website, Facebook, Twitter, or other media channel lively and up-to-date could be more than a small operation can take on. If you have to pick and choose, where should you focus your efforts?

Turns out that's an easy one: Your top priority has to be your own website. It really doesn't matter what you're raising money for: yourself, a friend, a team, a charity, an event—your website is your most valuable tool. So make sure it tells donors what they want to know (more on that below) before you turn your attention to composing pearls of wisdom in 140 characters or less.

Why's that? Because a majority of online donations come through charities' own websites. Network for Good, which processes donations and provides other services for nonprofits, follows the money that flows in to the more than 20,000 charities that use its platform. It consistently finds that 60 percent or more of the donations it handles come through charity websites, as shown in **Figure 4.1**, followed by charity portals and social websites.

Social media, on the other hand, is still in its infancy as a fundraising tool, although there have been some notable successes. The ShareCraft 2012—Save the Children Challenge FundRazr campaign has raised more than $1 million on Facebook for children in the Horn of Africa. Still, fewer than 1 percent of nonprofits have raised more than $100,000 using social media, according to the *2011 Nonprofit Social Network Benchmark Report* by NTEN, Common Knowledge, and Blackbaud. The real value in social media so far has been in building relationships and creating awareness about causes.

TIP: Don't use commercial Web-based email for your nonprofit business, suggests nonprofit coach Sandy Rees: "Your email needs to have your website domain address. Otherwise, you look a little fly-by-night."

Figure 4.1 *Dollars donated through charity websites increased 10 percent over 2010 and accounted for more than half of all donations through Network for Good in 2011.*

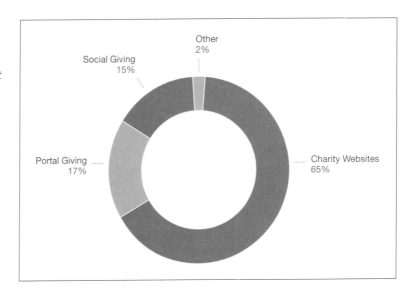

How to Show You're on the Ball

Another reason to lavish your website with love and care is that pretty much anyone who's half thinking about contributing money (or time, for that matter) to your organization is going to head straight to your homepage to do some research. Visitors will want to see signs that your group is trustworthy and well-run. If it's July and your homepage is all about last year's Thanksgiving coat drive, people might wonder if you're even around anymore. Not exactly confidence-inspiring.

Also, put yourself in your visitors' shoes. Ask yourself why people come to your website. What do they want to read or learn about? That's quite a different approach than just providing information you want them to know.

Here are some must-haves for an effective nonprofit website:

- Up-to-date content that instantly conveys what your organization does. Visitors don't want to plod through jargon or academic text. Make it easy to understand, and let your organization's personality come through!

- A moving story with a dramatic photo of someone you've helped. This should be the centerpiece that draws people in and lets them feel the impact of what you do (**Figure 4.2**). Remember what we said in Chapter 3: Giving is emotional. (See the sidebar for some storytelling pointers.)

Figure 4.2 *A photo that elicits an emotional reaction is a powerful tool for connecting with your website visitors.*

Credit: Liana Aghajanian/ CC-BY-SA-3.0

- Your address and phone number on every page, and complete contact info for your staff.

- A big, easy-to-find Donate button, ideally on the same spot on every page of your website. Tell visitors the difference their donation will make ("$25 will buy a nutritious lunch for 33 children.")

- An automated thank-you email to confirm donations.

- An address and downloadable donation form for people who prefer to give by mail.

- Clear information about where donations go—specific programs, people, or activities.

- Testimonials and ratings, such as from GuideStar and Charity Navigator.

- Information about how to get involved other than by donating. Can visitors volunteer? Make a gift? Conduct a drive? Attend an event?

- Links to your Twitter, Facebook, and other social media pages.

- A list of your board members.

TIP: If you haven't built your website yet and don't know where to start, check out some of the top open-source content management systems such as WordPress, Joomla, Plone, and Drupal, which are used by many nonprofits. For comparisons of these systems, go to Idealware at www.idealware.com.

After you've whipped your homepage into supporter-worthy shape, it's also worth your while to spend a little time on your donation page. According to Network for Good, its charity customers received significantly more donations and higher gifts when they put their own branding on their donation form, rather than using a generic form with Network for Good's branding (**Figure 4.3**).

Figure 4.3 *In 2011, Network for Good saw a 4 percent increase in average gift size for charities with a branded donation page, versus a 2 percent increase for those with a generic page.*
Source: Network for Good

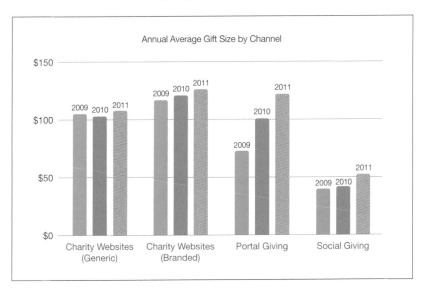

By now you should sense the importance of your website, and realize that keeping it fresh is a priority. Your Facebook and Twitter pages will take some tending too, so you'll need to decide if you have the resources to do them right. If you want to maximize your nonprofit presence on the Web, go to Chapter 9 for more on social media fundraising.

Industry INSIDER

 ## The Power of Storytelling

When you're trying to raise money, you want to highlight the impact of your organization, and the most powerful way to do that is through storytelling. Tell your story in a way that captures the heart and the emotion of the potential giver. Photos are important!

At its most basic, a compelling story that gains attention can be told in seven steps, including the following ideas. You don't have to use these exact words, of course, but try to include all of the elements in sequence.

1. Once upon a time … (Starts the story off, introduces the hero.)

2. And every day … (Sets up how life was before the incident.)

3. Until one day … (Begins the action of the story with the inciting incident and the goal.)

4. And because of this … (Introduces the barrier[s] the hero faces.)

5. And because of this … (Longer stories may have more than one.)

6. Until finally … (The resolution.)

7. And ever since that day … (Closing; what this means for the hero.)

For example, consider this fundraising "story:"

1. Mary seems to have it all. She lives with her husband and two children in a custom Mediterranean home in a close-knit neighborhood.

2. As a local grade-school teacher, Mary is well-known and liked throughout her town.

3. However, Mary and her husband have been increasingly living beyond their financial means, while trying to afford extensive medical care for their five-year-old daughter's chronic illness.

4. Their money troubles have just become critical this month as Mary's husband has experienced a job layoff.

5. And to further complicate money matters, their daughter's medical condition has taken a turn for the worse.

6. Mary has asked her worship community for emotional support, and she has received their generous help with everyday tasks like preparing meals and providing rides to the hospital.

7. Mary is very thankful for this immediate help, of course, but now she needs broader financial support from her community. That's why we've established our "Get Well, Amanda" charity fund in her daughter's name. Will you please help with a donation, too?

Online Fundraising Websites for Nonprofits and Donors

Following are just some of the top social sites for online fundraising. Generally speaking, they're set up so individuals and organizations can create fundraising pages and easily get the word out to their networks to reach more potential supporters. Fees and services may change, so check the websites for current information.

Causes

www.causes.com

GuideStar-verified 501(c)(3) nonprofits can collect donations through Causes. Users can create or join a cause to support an issue or nonprofit, and mobilize their networks to donate, recruit, and share to support the cause. Campaigns on Causes are automatically integrated with Facebook.

Fees: 4.75 percent transaction fee

CauseVox

www.causevox.com

CauseVox is an online fundraising company that serves small- to medium-size nonprofits. Its platform helps nonprofits create customized fundraising websites for campaigns as well as for personal and team fundraising. Instead of sending donors to another site for processing, CauseVox fundraising takes place on the nonprofit's own site.

Fees: No monthly fees until your organization raises $3,000; thereafter, $39 per month plus transaction fees of 7.5 percent to 8 percent plus 60 cents, depending on payment choice.

Crowdrise

www.crowdrise.com

Crowdrise combines online fundraising, crowdsourcing, social networking, contests, and more. Nonprofits can turn donors, supporters, and volunteers into fundraisers by asking them to create their own free fundraising pages on Crowdrise. Supporters can use their personal fundraising page to raise money from their friends and family.

Fees: For basic account, 5 percent plus $1 for donations under $25 and $2.50 for donations over $25; for featured account, $49 per month plus 4.95 percent Crowdrise fee and $1 transaction fee.

Donate Now/Network for Good

www.networkforgood.org

Network for Good helps nonprofits raise money on their own websites and on social networks with free and low-cost fundraising tools. It also enables giving to any charity registered in the United States at www.networkforgood.org, through fundraising widgets on social networks, and via partners' websites. Network for Good processes payments for thousands of nonprofit organizations.

Fees: For DonateNow Lite, 5 percent transaction fee; for standard Donate Now, $199 for setup, plus $49.95 per month and 3 percent transaction fee.

DonorsChoose

www.donorschoose.org

DonorsChoose.org is an online charity that makes it easy for anyone to help students in need. Public school teachers post requests, and individuals can give directly to the ones that inspire them. To date, 225,000 public and charter school teachers have used DonorsChoose.org to secure $111 million in books, art supplies, technology, and other resources that their students need to learn.

Fees: Shipping, fulfillment cost, and credit-card processing are added to the project cost. An optional 15 percent donation to DonorsChoose.org is suggested to donors at checkout.

FirstGiving

www.firstgiving.org

FirstGiving empowers individuals to raise money online for thousands of causes and helps 501(c)(3) nonprofit organizations plan, execute, and measure successful online fundraising campaigns. FirstGiving provides tools for charity fundraising events and grassroots fundraising campaigns and securely processes online donations.

Fees: 7.5 percent transaction fee

Fundly

www.fundly.com

Fundly is a social fundraising platform for individuals and organizations raising funds for nonprofits, charities, politics, schools, clubs, teams, groups, and others. It is designed to make it easy to fundraise via websites such as Facebook and Twitter. Supporters can reach out to their connections with branded tools, including email and social networking.

Fees: 4.9 percent transaction fee for individuals and organizations that raise less than $25,000 per month

Fundraise.com

www.fundraise.com

Fundraise.com allows anyone, or any organization, to create and manage all of their online fundraising activity. The platform provides an iPhone app, mobile-optimized website, Facebook and Twitter sharing, widgets, and a traditional website. Causes can be institutional, organizational, educational, political, personal, or faith-based.

Fees: 7.5 percent transaction fee

FundRazr

www.fundrazr.com

FundRazr is a social fundraising app for individuals, groups, nonprofits, and political causes. FundRazr includes the ability to share through

Facebook, social networks, email contacts, and websites or blogs to promote and collect money for causes.

Fees: 4.9 percent plus 30 cents per transaction

Givezooks!

www.givezooks.com

Nonprofit organizations can create custom campaigns, wish lists, grassroots fundraisers, and events online, expand donor outreach via social networking (Facebook and Twitter) and Internet marketing, and increase funds raised. To promote a campaign online, you can create custom landing pages and embeddable widgets to allow supporters and donors to help you spread the word by embedding them on their own pages.

Fees: Subscription fees start at $129 per month.

GoFundMe

www.gofundme.com

GoFundMe is a do-it-yourself online fundraising service with easy-to-use donation websites for weddings, graduations, accidents, illnesses, nonprofits, and charities.

Fees: For PayPal, 5 percent transaction fee plus processing fee of 2.9 percent plus 30 cents; for WePay, 3.5 percent plus 50 cents.

Help Attack!

www.helpattack.com

Using either Twitter or Facebook, donors make a monetary pledge to their favorite cause, giving with each action they take on their preferred social network over 30 days. For example, a donor can pledge 10 cents per tweet or Facebook update. After 30 days, pledges are calculated and donations are sent to the nonprofit of the donor's choice.

Fees: 8.5 percent transaction fee

Indiegogo

www.indiegogo.com

Indiegogo was launched in 2008 to provide any idea (creative, cause, or entrepreneurial) with the tools and process to raise money and offer perks. Social media integration, direct email, and announcement features make it easy to spread the word, raise awareness, and increase funding.

Fees: 4 percent fee if a funding goal is met; 9 percent if not; credit card fees are approximately 3 percent.

JustGive

www.justgive.org

Through JustGive, donors can give to nonprofit organizations through direct and memorial donations, charity gift cards, charity wedding registries, gift collections, and fundraising registries. Nonprofits can get a Donate Now button for their website, promote their fundraisers on Facebook and Twitter, create email campaigns, and track donations.

Fees: 4.5 percent transaction fee

Pay It Square

www.payitsquare.com

Fundraisers can create a customized page, promote their fundraiser, and collect donations online, including on Facebook. Organizers can easily track pledges and offline contributions as well.

Fees: 99-cent transaction fee plus PayPal fees; for a credit-card payment, 2.9 percent plus 30 cents.

Razoo

www.razoo.com

Razoo allows you to create team fundraising pages as well as pages at the organizational level. You can accept donations on your own website using an embeddable widget that donors can also use to embed on their own sites with a click. It also offers template-driven event pages you can use for individual fundraising events.

Fees: 2.9 percent transaction fee

StayClassy

www.stayclassy.org

StayClassy is a software platform for small- and medium-size nonprofits. It offers event management for any type of event, the ability to accept online donations, reporting and analytics, and individual and team fundraising pages.

Fees: Monthly fees start at $49 plus transaction fee and credit card fee.

Helping Hand

Some points to remember about the multitude of options available for online fundraising:

- Nonprofits can have an online presence on their own website, social giving websites, charity portals, and social media websites.

- Nonprofits should make their website a top priority, because that's where most online donations come from.

- The most effective element of a nonprofit website is a story (with photos) of someone they've helped.

Up next in Chapter 5, we'll share the "101" of online fundraising operations.

Part 2

ONLINE
FUNDRAISING
OPERATIONS

5

Lay the Groundwork for Fundraising

One of the many appealing aspects of online fundraising is its speed. You can set up a widget or a page on a social fundraising website and start collecting donations literally within minutes. That's a big advantage in cases of immediate need—raising money for an emergency vet bill, for example, or a family who lost all their belongings in a fire.

Nonprofits, however, need to be careful not to get ahead of themselves. Fundraising, whether online or offline, should be part of a well-thought-out plan that directly aligns with your organization's mission and goals.

Are You Ready to Fundraise?

It's not unheard-of for a small nonprofit to look around at all the big guys online and decide that—if that's the latest and greatest way to make money—they want to be a part of it too. They add a PayPal Donate button (see Chapter 2) or sign up with Network for Good to process payments, and then...well, nothing much happens. So maybe online fundraising isn't all it's cracked up to be?

Not exactly.

In those situations, it's a good bet that the organizations started fundraising online before they had laid the proper groundwork. And as nonprofit experts are fond of saying, online fundraising is not a case of "if you build it, they will come."

NOTE: Section 501(c)(3) of the Internal Revenue Code grants tax exemptions to "corporations organized and operated exclusively for religious, charitable, scientific, testing for public safety, literary, or educational purposes, or to foster national or international amateur sports, or prevention of cruelty for children or animals." This status gives tax breaks not only to the organizations, but also to their supporters, whose donations are tax-deductible.

Before we move on to online considerations, ask yourself these questions to assess whether your organization is ready for *any* type of fundraising yet:

- Do you have legal permission to fundraise? Check with your state Attorney General's Office and your local authorities for requirements, and see Chapter 6 for more information on legal matters.

- Does your organization have 501(c)(3) status (see Note) or a fiscal sponsor so you can solicit tax-exempt donations?

- Do you have a clear mission statement?

- Do you have a strong case statement that answers these key questions: Why should someone give to your organization? Why is your cause important? What is your timeline? (See the sidebar for a sample case statement.)

- Do you have a budget detailing your income and expenses? (See **Table 5.1** for a sample budget.)

- Have you explored partnerships with local businesses, corporations, and government programs?

- Do you have a fundraising plan mapping out one-year goals? Five-year goals?

- Do you have a core group of supporters who will actively fundraise for you?

- Do you have a database or other method of tracking donors?

- Do you have the people and technology you need to get your donations into the bank and to thank your donors promptly?

- Do you have a communication plan for your donors (newsletters, annual report, holiday cards, progress updates)?

Industry INSIDER

 ### A Sample Fundraising Case Statement

Fundraising coach, consultant, and author Sandy Rees, at www.getfullyfunded.com, specializes in working with small nonprofits. She uses this template to help her clients write a case statement:

Your case statement is a summary of the reason(s) for people to give. You should have a case statement for your organization, and one for individual programs or projects.

Before you attempt to craft a case statement, you may find it helpful to collect a copy of each of your organization's materials, like previous case statements, brochures, annual reports, newsletters, direct mail letters, and grant proposals. Often, you can reuse the information.

1. What is your organization's mission statement? It needs to be short, concise, and compelling.

2. What problem does your organization address? (Feed the hungry, help the sick, house homeless animals, protect the environment, etc.)

3. How many people are affected by this problem in the area you serve?

4. Briefly describe your organization's history.

5. What success has your organization had in addressing the problem?

6. What success stories can you tell about the people you've helped?

7. What need are you raising money for?

8. What is the fundraising goal for this need?

9. How will the donor's gift affect the need?

10. What makes the need urgent? (Why should the donor give *now*?)

The following table shares a simple version of Sandy Rees's fundraising budget template. If you prefer more detail, break down each category by month.

Table 5.1 Sample Budget Template

Revenue	Last Year Actual	Coming Year Budget	Difference
Grants			
Special events			
General public contributions			
Direct mail			
Major gifts			
Newsletter			
Total			

Expenses	Last Year Actual	Coming Year Budget	Difference
Printing and copying			
Postage			
Special event expenses			
Donor and volunteer appreciation			
Travel and meetings			
Staff and volunteer training			
Contract services			
Miscellaneous			
Total			
Difference			

Making the Move to Online Fundraising

That's a long to-do list, and it's understandable if it feels overwhelming. But that's the reality of running a nonprofit. Fundraising may be a straightforward goal, but it's a complex effort that requires financial skills, persuasion skills, committed personnel, technological know-how, and spot-on communications.

If you remain undaunted, it's time to assess the next phase of fundraising readiness: knowing when to move online. You'll want to have the tasks above well in hand, because those are some of the items that will help shape your all-important website.

As for your website, here are a couple of tasks to do from an organizational standpoint:

Decide who's in charge. The person who manages your website (we're guessing it's you) will have to commit to updating it every month or so to give visitors a reason to keep coming back. If you don't have the skills, delegate to a friend or a volunteer or a staffer, if you have one. Be sure they know it's a must-do, not a nice-to-do. Remember, your website is the most important piece of your online fundraising strategy, so treat it as a true priority.

Invest in the right tools (and budget accordingly). It's absolutely essential that online donors receive an automated email confirmation of their gift as soon as it goes through—be sure your payment processor offers that feature. You also might need donor management software, or an email marketing service to send newsletters. Costs can vary widely, so do some research and get recommendations from other organizations your size. You might find it worth the money to pay someone to do the initial setup of your website, a cost that can run from the hundreds into the thousands of dollars, depending on features.

TIP: The Nonprofit Technology Network (NTEN) and Idealware, a nonprofit that researches software for other nonprofits, compared 29 donor management systems that cost $4,000 or less in the first year. Their report, "A Consumers Guide to Low Cost Donor Management Systems," is available free at www.nten.org/research/2011-dms.

Planning an Online Fundraising Campaign

Now that you have all the pieces in place, it's time to get down to business and outline your fundraising plan, which will be a mix of online and offline activities. We talked about the elements of an effective website in Chapter 4, but it bears repeating: Tell emotionally moving stories that show people how their money will make an impact. Make it easy for supporters to donate, volunteer, or sign up for your newsletter. If you have a blog, Facebook page, or Twitter account, link to those, too. In turn, you can use Facebook and Twitter to drive traffic back to your website. Include your mailing address and phone number on every Web page.

Your fundraising plan should also include:

Email newsletters. Every month and a half or so, send a newsletter to donors and prospects. Build your email list through sign-ups on your website, collecting email addresses at events, and asking for them over the phone. We'll talk more about newsletter content in Chapter 7.

Integrating online and offline efforts. Drive traffic to your website by putting your Web address on your business cards, direct mail pieces, brochures—any materials you produce. Send an email in advance of a mailing to tell supporters it's on the way, and offer the option of donating directly from the email.

Special campaigns. Plan a December fundraising drive to tap into the biggest giving days of the year. In spring, consider holding an event. Or, if your cause has a month associated with it, like October for breast cancer research donations, use that as your fundraising hook.

Tracking. Use analytics tools to determine which pages and articles on your website performed well (or not so well.) Armed with that information, you'll know what to write for your next update or what to feature most prominently. Google Analytics provides a wealth of data for free, and is sufficient for most small nonprofits. Your Web host most likely offers basic analytics, too.

You Have to "Ask"

Another one of the unique benefits of online fundraising is that it spares you the potentially awkward task of asking people for money face-to-face. Mind you, you still have to develop that skill, but it takes a different form online.

The online "ask" is likely going to be based on an emotional homepage story and photo, as we talked about in the previous chapter. Here's a typical kind of ask: "For the first time since he entered kindergarten, Alex now has a backpack filled with the supplies he needs to succeed in school. Your gift of $30 today will help another student stay on the path to college."

In your email newsletter highlighting the backpack drive, consider writing a profile of a donor, and why that particular cause captured her attention.

As with everything on your website, you want to make it easy for donors to give. Your Donate button should be easy to find, and "above the fold," meaning visitors don't have to scroll to find it. When supporters get to the donation page, don't break the mood by making them fill out unnecessary form fields (people get especially hesitant about required phone numbers.)

BY THE NUMBERS

 ### Volunteering

According to the U.S. Bureau of Labor Statistics, approximately **26.8 percent of Americans** over the age of 16 volunteered through or for an organization between September 2010 and September 2011. This proportion has remained relatively constant since 2003, after a slight increase from 27.4 percent to 28.8 percent in 2003.

Keep in mind that not everyone who comes to your website will be prepared to give. Most people go to charities' websites to do some research before they donate. These are the so-called "happy bystanders" on the ladder of engagement (see discussion on the next page)—in effect, they're willing to listen but haven't quite made up their minds.

For them, a different kind of "ask" is in order. Let them know how they can engage with you in nonfinancial ways: by volunteering, attending an event, or telling their friends about your organization.

Suggest an amount. If $30 will cover half of the backpack supplies, suggest that, but leave room for an amount of the donor's choosing. And speaking of choice, be sure to include a monthly giving option.

Understanding the "Ladder of Engagement"

In the nonprofit world, the "ladder of engagement" is a concept that describes people's level of commitment to a cause. Your supporters most likely will hop around the rungs to a degree, but the idea is to deepen your connection with them and move them up the ladder over time (**Figure 5.1**).

Beth Kanter, coauthor of *The Networked Nonprofit* and author of the popular Beth's Blog at www.bethkanter.org, says organizations' communication and relationship-building strategies should help move people through the various roles and levels of involvement.

"They don't all move, it isn't linear, and it's messy," she says. "Very important is the network weaving done by the personal fundraiser who inspires, connects, and motivates people in the campaign."

Figure 5.1 *The ladder of engagement shows the range of involvement people feel toward causes they support.*

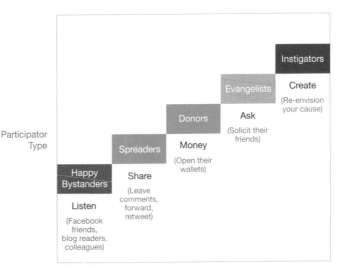

Here are the players involved in the ladder of engagement:

- **Happy bystanders:** Blog readers, Facebook friends, offline colleagues.

- **Spreaders:** People who are willing to share the information about your cause with other people. They may add the widget to their profile, retweet, leave a comment on someone's blog, Digg your post, bookmark it, forward a video to friends, and so on.

- **Donors:** Open their wallets.

- **Evangelists:** Solicit their friends on your behalf.

- **Instigators:** Create their own version of your cause and why it is meaningful to them.

Keep the ladder of engagement in mind as you develop your communication and fundraising plans. Ideally, your website will appeal to visitors no matter where they are on the ladder. Think about the kinds of content (favorable ratings, testimonials, success stories) that might bump a happy bystander up to the donor level.

By contrast, instigators have already donated, so you don't need to sell them on your organization's value. They might be looking for information about leadership opportunities or your next big campaign.

PayPal INSIDER

 ### eBay Giving Works: Three Ways to Fundraise

eBay Giving Works offers convenient and trusted ways for people to give to nonprofits:

- eBay sellers can donate a percentage of their items' final sale prices to nonprofits that are registered with the program. Buyers can purchase these items, identified by a distinctive blue-and-yellow ribbon, or add a minimum $1 donation at checkout to eBay purchases paid through PayPal.

- Nonprofits can sell their own goods on eBay for free to raise funds.

- Any eBay member can make a direct cash donation through PayPal at any time, with no obligation to buy or sell.

At the close of 2011, eBay sellers and buyers had raised nearly $300 million for nonprofits in the United States, Canada, and the United Kingdom since eBay Giving Works was launched in 2003.

For more information, go to www.ebaygivingworks.com.

Industry INSIDER

 ## How to Raise Money Without Asking for Money

GoodSearch.com CEO Scott Garell came up with eight ways for nonprofits to ask supporters to raise money without writing a check:

1. Shop online: Ask supporters to start their online shopping at GoodShop. GoodShop is a shopping portal that donates a percentage of almost every purchase from more than 2,500 stores (including Gap, Target, Staples, and Macy's) to your organization. You sign up on the website, and your supporters designate you as their recipient.

2. Recycle electronics: Hold a gadget drive where supporters bring in their old electronics (including smartphones, laptops, iPods, and more) and you turn them in for cash through eBay Instant Sale or other buyback programs.

3. Redeem credit card points. Ask members to turn their unused credit card points into a charitable donation. Both American Express and Citibank offer this program.

4. Search the Internet: GoodSearch.com is a Yahoo!-powered search engine that donates about a penny per search to your cause after you sign up.

5. Meet someone: Partner with a local bar, restaurant, or retailer. You send people to their establishment, and each time someone "checks in" there on a social networking website such as Foursquare, the establishment donates to your cause.

6. Donate airline and hotel miles: Most airlines allow people to use their frequent flier miles to buy tickets or office items for other people. Ask your supporters to use theirs to help your organization.

7. Dine out: GoodDining.com gives up to 6 percent of the money spent on a meal at 10,000 restaurants across the country to the diner's cause of choice.

8. Volunteer: A handful of companies match volunteer hours with funds. For example, Microsoft matches volunteer time at $17 an hour. Boeing, Exxon, Intel, Chevron, and Bank of America have similar programs.

Helping Hand

Online fundraising can be set up quickly, but you definitely don't want to be slapdash about it. Follow these pointers for success:

- Assess your overall readiness for fundraising. Recognize that online fundraising takes commitment.

- Plan a campaign that integrates online and offline fundraising methods.

- Craft an online "ask" that resonates with people who are already inclined to give and those who just want to get to know your organization better.

Coming in Chapter 6, we'll go through the legal and ethical issues that come up in online fundraising.

6

Keep Your Legal House in Order

Some aspects of online fundraising are especially exciting. The little thrill when an email notifies you of another donation, the satisfaction of seeing your thermometer creep ever closer toward your goal—those are fun, rewarding reminders of your hard work.

But along with the fun comes a healthy dose of housekeeping to be filed under "dull but important." There are legal requirements that you absolutely have to meet (tax forms! registrations!) so you can get and keep your tax-exempt status.

Let's go over those, along with some ethical guidelines, to help you earn—and maintain—your donors' trust.

Guidelines for Individuals

We've focused a lot in this book on the work of small nonprofits because they're such prolific fundraisers. But we haven't forgotten that millions of people each year launch individual fundraising drives that aren't affiliated with a nonprofit organization. Often these are short-term efforts for the scenarios we've mentioned before: raising money for someone who's sick or suffered a loss in a fire or accident or other crisis.

It's perfectly legal for an individual to raise money and for a recipient to accept it—you don't have to be a 501(c)(3) nonprofit organization to solicit such donations.

NONPROFIT SUCCESS STORY

 ### A Life-Changing Campaign for a Bullied Bus Monitor

An unprecedented example of individual fundraising is the case of Karen Klein, the 68-year-old New York bus monitor whose bullying by seventh-grade boys was captured on video and posted on YouTube in June 2012.

Max Sidorov of Toronto saw the video and set up a 30-day campaign on Indiegogo to raise $5,000 to send Klein on a nice vacation (**Figure 6.1**). Within three days, the fund ballooned past $600,000, with a final tally just shy of $704,000—more than 45 times her annual salary of $15,506 and enough for her to quit her bus job and retire.

Because the donations were gifts, that astonishing windfall is tax free for Klein. The 32,000-plus donations aren't tax deductible for donors because they went to an individual, not a nonprofit. According to

Indiegogo, the average contribution amount was $21, and the most frequent amount was $10. The highest single contribution was $3,000.

Figure 6.1 *Max Sidorov's individual fundraising campaign for New York bus monitor Karen Klein raised almost $704,000.*

Credit: Lori A. Coleman, Photographer & Designer, LIGHT+INK

The IRS considers income from donations to be a nontaxable personal gift to the recipient. It's actually donors, not recipients, who pay gift taxes, but those don't kick in unless someone gives more than $13,000 to an individual in a given year. We're not tax experts, so talk to your tax adviser about your specific situation.

When you raise money for an individual though, you'll need to make sure donors understand that their contributions aren't tax deductible, as they would be if they were funneled through a nonprofit. This probably won't matter within a small circle of donors—an accident victim's friends and coworkers, for example—but if you solicit a broader group, it's likely that some people will want to know if their contribution is deductible.

TIP: Donations to qualified charities are tax deductible, but only if donors itemize their deductions on Form 1040, Schedule A. Payments to individuals are never deductible. IRS Publication 526, Charitable Contributions, has complete information.

Individuals as well as nonprofits can accept payments online through a PayPal Donate button—again, it's not only for charities. Individuals just pay regular PayPal fees rather than the discounted nonprofit rate. GoFundMe, Fundly, FundRazr, and other services are also set up for individual fundraisers (see the Resources in the Appendix for more information).

Some payment services, including PayPal, may limit the amount of money account holders can send, especially for new accounts. Check your service's policies so you don't encounter unnecessary delays when you transfer donations to the recipient.

Complete and Maintain Required Forms

If you have your hard-won 501(c)(3) tax-exempt status, it means that you've made it through a considerable (and possibly somewhat painful) process at both the state and federal levels.

States approve nonprofit status, while tax exemptions are governed by federal law. Once you're declared a 501(c)(3)—basically a public charity or a private foundation—not only is your organization exempt from federal and (most likely) state taxes, but your supporters' donations are tax deductible as well.

Here are six major benefits of 501(c)(3) status:

1. Exemption from federal income tax

2. Tax-deductible contributions for donors

3. Possible exemption from state income, sales, and employment taxes

4. Reduced postal rates

5. Exemption from federal unemployment tax

6. Tax-exempt financing

TIP: If you haven't applied for tax-exempt status, or if you want more information on how to maintain it, you can visit a specialty website the IRS created for 501(c)(3) organizations. IRS Stay Exempt at www.stayexempt.org contains sections on new organizations, existing organizations, and in-depth topics.

You've probably done some offline fundraising, so we'll assume you're registered with the Attorney General's Office in your home state, and any local jurisdictions as required.

When you extend your fundraising online, though, you trigger yet another layer of bureaucracy, because the beauty of being able to collect donations from people in other states means, well, you'll be collecting donations from people in other states. And that means you have to comply with those states' regulations *before* you start fundraising.

The same tools that make it so easy for the good guys like you to raise money for worthy causes also make it easy for the bad guys to pull off scams under the guise of charity. Attorneys General, naturally, work hard to prevent that, so in most states they require at least baseline information about any organization that collects money from their citizens. Can't blame them for that, right?

Registering isn't quite as onerous as it could be, thanks to a form called the Unified Registration Statement, available at www.multistatefiling.org. Two agencies—the National Association of State Charities Officials and the National Association of Attorneys General—created the form so non-profits could register with multiple states (currently 36 plus the District of Columbia) at once.

Three states (Colorado, Florida, and Oklahoma) don't accept the form, and the rest don't require registration. Yet another condition to track: Some states require one-time registration only, while others require annual renewal. (If your donations from residents of a particular state total less than $5,000 a year, or other designated amount, you could be exempt from registering in that state. Check the state's guidelines to be sure.)

No question, it's complicated, so someone in your organization will have to pay close attention.

Satisfy the Feds, Too

The number of 501(c)(3) charities in the United States dropped from 1.28 million to 1.08 million from 2010 to 2011 (**Figure 6.2**) as a result of a 2006 requirement that even small nonprofits file reporting documents with the IRS. In 2011 more than 200,000 charities lost their tax-exempt status for not filing Form 990 for three consecutive years. Most are believed to be small organizations that were defunct.

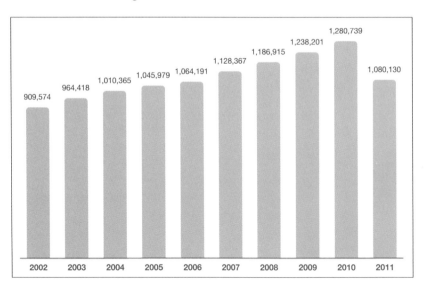

Figure 6.2 *The number of 501(c)(3) charities in the United States dropped from 1.28 million to 1.08 million from 2010 to 2011*

Credit: GivingUSA Foundation

While 501(c)(3) status exempts your organization from taxes, it doesn't exempt you from having to file certain information each year with the IRS (unless your gross receipts are less than $5,000, or you're a qualified religious organization—then you're off the hook). Don't skip filing if you think you're too small for Uncle Sam to notice, because (a) he'll notice, and (b) failure to file three years in a row is grounds for revoking your tax-exempt status (Figure 6.2). To be reinstated, you'd have the hassle and expense of starting the whole application process again from scratch.

So then, how do you keep your nonprofit's nose clean? Get to know and love IRS Form 990. Organizations with gross receipts of $50,000 or less file the 990-N, an electronic e-postcard that asks for the following eight pieces of information:

1. Employer identification number (EIN), also known as a Taxpayer Identification Number (TIN)

2. Tax year

3. Legal name and mailing address

4. Any other names the organization uses

5. Name and address of a principal officer

6. Website address, if the organization has one

7. Confirmation that the organization's annual gross receipts are $50,000 or less for tax years ending on or after December 31, 2010

8. If applicable, a statement that the organization has terminated or is terminating (going out of business)

If your gross average receipts are higher than $50,000, you'll file either a Form 990 or 990-EZ.

TIP: The IRS has an online workshop about the Form 990 that covers recordkeeping, filing, and what happens during an audit. It's available at http://www.stayexempt.irs.gov/VirtualWorkshop/Form990.aspx.

Ethical Conduct Builds Trust

Honoring legal obligations is one way for nonprofits to demonstrate their commitment to conducting business with integrity. Equally important are an organization's ethical standards.

When donors give to a charity, especially online, they're placing their trust in you on several levels. Of course they trust that their donation will be spent the way they intend, but they also trust you with personal information and possibly financial information. It's up to you as an organization to respect donors' privacy and security, and to prove yourself a worthy steward of their gifts.

Let's examine some of the ethical issues that are especially relevant in the online arena.

Privacy

Email addresses are extremely valuable in fundraising, so nonprofits are wise to gather them on their website, at events, during phone calls—wherever they can.

But if you sell your mailing list and your constituents are suddenly inundated with spam—or worse, if you blast them with too many emails yourself—you're going to turn off the very people you're courting.

To allay their concerns, tell them on your sign-up form how you will and won't use their email address (hint: don't sell it).

Note also that nonprofits are subject to the federal CAN-SPAM act. Follow these rules and you'll be in good shape legally and ethically:

- Your "From," "To," "Reply-To," and routing information—including the originating domain name and email address—must be accurate and identify you or your organization as the sender.

- The subject line must accurately reflect the content of the message.

- Clearly identify the message as an ad (marketing) if the recipient is likely to view it that way.

- Your message must include your valid physical postal address: your street address, PO Box, or commercial mailbox.

- Tell recipients how to opt out of future emails. Give a return email address or an unsubscribe link in the email footer to allow people to communicate their choice to you. You can create a menu so they can opt out of certain types of messages, but you must include the option of stopping all emails.

- You must honor opt-out requests within 10 business days.

Be clear with supporters about how you might use their information. Obviously their giving history and details shouldn't be shared with anyone who doesn't have a specific need to know.

But you might want to draft a website privacy policy to address other scenarios, such as posting photos of donor events, listing donors' names on a thank-you page, or posting detailed meeting minutes with names of speakers. Offer an opt-out for those cases, too.

Security

Data security breaches still make news all too frequently, so it's understandable that not everyone is completely comfortable using a credit card online.

For a small nonprofit, the easiest approach is to engage a professional payment processor. That way you can assure your donors that their credit card transactions comply with Payment Card Industry (PCI) security standards (see sidebar), and that you don't store their credit card numbers in your database.

Transparency

Another way to build trust in your organization is to be transparent about your finances.

One of the requirements for 501(c)(3) charities is that they make their Form 990 available for public inspection.

Why not post it online, where it's available to anyone, 24/7? You can do the same with your annual report, audited financial statements, and IRS letter documenting your tax-exempt status.

Will anyone actually read them? Not as much as your gripping homepage tales, perhaps, but even so, these small gestures convey organizational openness and accountability that donors appreciate.

Stewardship

Kivi Leroux Miller, a blogger and president of Nonprofit Marketing Guide. com, conducts an experiment she calls "What I Got When I Gave," where she donates $25 to 10 national nonprofits at the end of the year, and then monitors how long it takes each group to acknowledge her unsolicited gift. One year, Miller received only three thank-yous after more than a month.

Take that as a powerful lesson in how *not* to treat your donors.

Stewardship is much more than saying thank you, of course. It's about nurturing your relationship with donors on a personal level. That means spending their contributions wisely, letting them know how their gifts were used, keeping them informed about your plans, and perhaps even inviting them to meet those whom their donations have helped.

Industry INSIDER

 PCI Compliance Requirements

Have you ever heard of the Payment Card Industry Data Security Standard, or PCI DSS? It's a set of requirements to ensure that all companies that process, store, or transmit credit card data maintain a secure environment. Essentially, PCI DSS is a security standard designed to make sure that consumer credit card data is not compromised.

If you have a merchant credit card account, you're required to become PCI compliant, which includes completing an annual self-assessment and quarterly system scans. Jumping through those hoops costs time and money. (You pay for the system scans.)

However, if you use services like PayPal Payments Standard or Express Checkout for all your credit card processing, your burden of complying with PCI standard is simplified. That's because you never see your customers' credit card data; your customers transmit their credit card information directly to PayPal. You don't have to take the time or spend the money to handle all the PCI compliance requirements—and your customers experience a safer transaction.

The exception to this process is if you handle your own credit card data, and use PayPal only for payment authorization via services for PayPal Payments Pro or Virtual Terminal. In this instance, you still need to ensure your own PCI compliance, as customers' credit card data passes through your hands.

In fact, according to research by Penelope Burk, author of *Donor-Centered Fundraising*, one of the main reasons donors stop giving is because they don't like the way they were treated after they gave. Some cite inadequate communication about where their money is going, or too-frequent appeals, but in many cases, donors—like Leroux Miller—didn't feel they were adequately thanked.

Be sure to show your gratitude by sending donors a thank-you letter within a few days of receiving a gift. Personalize your note as much as you can: Address the person by name (spell it right!) and refer to the specific gift amount, or the event that inspired the gift. Consider enclosing a photo or a short anecdote about a client. Sign the letter in ink. And whatever you do, don't use the thank-you to ask for another donation.

Katya Andresen of Network for Good recommends thanking donors three times for every one time you ask for money. Even if you don't quite achieve that rate, always say thank you promptly and sincerely, and you'll continue building relationships.

A Code of Ethics

Network for Good, which provides online fundraising services and resources for nonprofits, offers the following guidelines to promote high ethical standards for online fundraisers and marketers.

PHILANTHROPIC EXPERIENCE

1. Clearly and specifically display and describe the organization's identity on the organization's website.

2. Employ practices on the website that exhibit integrity, honesty, and truthfulness and seek to safeguard the public trust.

PRIVACY AND SECURITY

1. Seek to inspire trust in every online transaction.

2. Prominently display the opportunity for supporters to have their names removed from lists that are sold to, rented to, or exchanged with other organizations.

3. Conduct online transactions through a system that employs high-level security technology to protect the donor's personal information for both internal and external authorized use.

4. Provide an opt-in or opt-out mechanism to prevent unsolicited communications or solicitations by organizations that obtain email addresses directly from the donor. Should lists be rented or exchanged, only those verified as having been obtained through donors or prospects opting in will be used by a charity.

Industry INSIDER

 ### The Donor Bill of Rights

According to the Association of Fundraising Professionals, philanthropy is based on voluntary action for the common good. It is a tradition of giving and sharing that is primary to the quality of life. To ensure that philanthropy merits the respect and trust of the general public, and that donors and prospective donors can have full confidence in the nonprofit organizations and causes they are asked to support, the Association of Fundraising Professionals declares that all donors have the following rights:

1. To be informed of the organization's mission, of the way the organization intends to use donated resources, and of its capacity to use donations effectively for their intended purposes.

2. To be informed of the identity of those serving on the organization's governing board, and to expect the board to exercise prudent judgment in its stewardship responsibilities.

3. To have access to the organization's most recent financial statements.

4. To be assured that their gifts will be used for the purposes for which they were given.

5. To receive appropriate acknowledgement and recognition.

6. To be assured that information about their donation is handled with respect and with confidentiality to the extent provided by law.

7. To expect that all relationships with individuals representing organizations of interest to the donor will be professional in nature.

8. To be informed whether those seeking donations are volunteers, employees of the organization, or hired solicitors.

9. To have the opportunity for their names to be deleted from mailing lists that an organization may intend to share.

10. To feel free to ask questions when making a donation and to receive prompt, truthful, and forthright answers.

5. Protect the interests and privacy of individuals interacting with the organization's website.

6. Provide a clear, prominent, and easily accessible privacy policy on the organization's website telling visitors, at a minimum, what information is being collected, how it is being collected, how it can be updated or removed, how it will be used, and who has access to the data.

DISCLOSURES

1. Disclose the identity of the organization or provider processing an online transaction.

2. Guarantee that the name, logo, and likeness of all parties to an online transaction belong to the party and will not be used without express permission.

3. Maintain all appropriate governmental and regulatory designations .or certifications.

4. Provide both online and offline contact information.

TRANSACTIONS

1. Ensure that contributions are used to support the activities of the organization to which they were donated.

2. Ensure that legal control of contributions or proceeds from online transactions are transferred directly to the charity or expedited in the fastest possible way.

3. Ensure that companies providing online services to the organization provide clear and full communication on all aspects of donor transactions, including the accurate and timely transmission of data related to online transactions.

4. Stay informed regarding the best methods to ensure the ethical, secure, and private nature of online donations.

5. Adhere to the spirit as well as the letter of all applicable laws and regulations, including, but not limited to, charitable solicitation and tax laws.

6. Ensure that all services, recognition, and other transactions promised on a website, in consideration of [a] gift or transaction, will be fulfilled on a timely basis.

7. Disclose to the donor the nature of the relationship between the organization processing the gift or transaction and the charity intended to benefit from the gift.

Helping Hand

In summary, tax-exempt status has numerous advantages for nonprofit organizations and their donors, but it also brings with it a lot of record-keeping responsibilities to bear in mind, including:

- Nonprofits that bring in more than $5,000 a year must file a Form 990 with the IRS. Organizations that don't file for three consecutive years can have their tax-exempt status revoked.

- If you expect to receive donations from people outside your home state, you'll need to register with those states before you fundraise. A form called the Unified Registration Statement allows you to register with multiple states at once.

- Ethical conduct is essential to building and maintaining donors' trust. Show them that you respect their privacy and treat their financial information securely. Be open with information about your organization. Thank donors promptly and genuinely, and let them know how their gifts are making a difference.

Starting with Chapter 7, we'll begin a more in-depth look at the types of online fundraising, starting with email campaigns.

Part 3

ONLINE
FUNDRAISING
MEDIA

7

Fundraising Beyond the Homepage

Legal and IRS compliance? Check.

Inviting homepage with fresh content? Check.

Clean, easy-to-use Donate page? Check.

When you're satisfied that those top priorities are in tip-top shape, that's a sign that you're ready to turn your attention to the next phases of fundraising: email campaigns and some carefully chosen direct mailings to bolster your online efforts.

Either of these elements can become quite involved for even medium-size nonprofits. We'll outline a scaled-back plan that's more manageable for small shops.

Email: Versatile and Valuable

Email has a lot going for it as a fundraising tool. It's a personal, informal medium that most people are comfortable using. For nonprofits, it's an inexpensive way to communicate—you don't have the production and mailing costs of printed materials, or the hassles of stuffing envelopes and then cashing checks when they come in.

Email also is an invaluable tool for stewardship. You can keep your donors up to date on your programs and plans, thank them, share success stories, and invite their feedback.

Because email is so effective, your mailing list is possibly your organization's most valuable asset, other than your name and reputation. Researchers have even calculated how much an email address is worth. *The Convio Online Marketing Nonprofit Benchmark Index™ Study* for 2011, which looked at 700 nonprofits in the United States and Canada, found that the median amount raised per usable email address was $12.92 in 2011, up from $12.48 in 2010 and $11.68 in 2009 (**Figure 7.1**).

Figure 7.1 *The median amount raised per usable email address per year across all verticals was $12.92 in 2011, a small but continued increase.*

Source: Convio

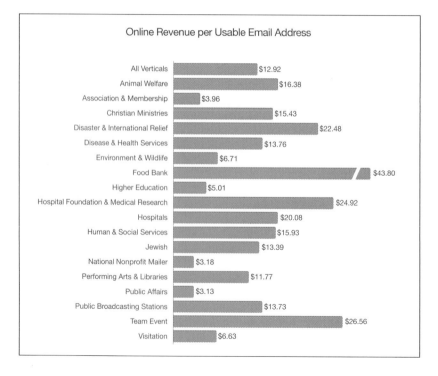

It follows, then, that you'll want to be proactive about building your email list. Here are some ideas for collecting email addresses:

- **From your website:** Place a Subscribe button on your homepage, or better yet, on every page of your website. It can be as simple for your visitors as just submitting their email address. If you want to collect more information with a longer form, make it easy by asking for only the information you really need—name, email address, home address. You can always gather phone numbers or information on personal interests later. Tell supporters why they'd want to subscribe: "Sign up for our e-newsletter and get news, tips, and updates on how you're making a difference in our community."

- **Offer an incentive:** Enter new subscribers into a drawing to win a gift certificate or other modest prize. If you conduct research or write tip sheets or white papers, offer them as free downloads. Put a quiz or puzzle on your homepage.

- **On social media:** Add a sign-up form to your Facebook page.

- **From direct-mail pieces:** Include a line for email addresses on donation forms that are mailed in.

- **From phone calls:** Ask for email addresses when you call your supporters. You can mention that email communication saves your nonprofit time and money.

- **In your office:** Place an email sign-up sheet at your reception desk for people who visit you in person.

- **From business cards:** When you exchange business cards at conferences or other functions, be sure to enter the email addresses into your database. Put a bowl or basket in your office to collect business cards.

- **From your email signature:** Include a link to your sign-up form in your own email signature.

- **At events:** Place a sign-up sheet at your fundraisers, or in your booth at community outreach events.

- **From current supporters:** Include a "forward to a friend" link in your e-newsletter.

- **Ask donors:** On your donation form, ask supporters for the email address of one or two other people who might be interested in your cause.

Once you have a nice base of email subscribers, it's on to the next challenges: What are you going to write about? What if writing isn't your strongest skill? What if your organization is so small that you don't need, or can't afford, an email service and a professional e-newsletter?

DIY vs. Email Services

Let's get the last one out of the way first: There's nothing wrong with sending plain-text emails. Nicely designed newsletters with several articles are great, but they're not a must, especially for small organizations. Your supporters aren't looking to be entertained or dazzled by visuals—they just want to know that their contributions are making an impact. You can accomplish that just fine with periodic text emails.

If you're really on a shoestring budget or you're just starting out, you could set yourself up on Google Groups or Yahoo! Groups for free, ask your supporters to subscribe to your group, and send your emails from there.

PRODUCT SPOTLIGHT

 Email Services

Groundwire, an online communications and technology consulting shop, evaluates email services to provide a baseline for its clients. In its *Comparison of Email Service Providers 2012* report, Groundwire classified services by technical expertise required:

Services geared toward nontechnical users

- MailChimp
- Campaign Monitor
- iContact

- Constant Contact
- VerticalResponse
- Network for Good
- Emma

Services geared toward more technical users

- WhatCounts
- ExactTarget
- JangoMail
- Predictive Response

That said, email services offer features that can make your life easier, at prices starting around $30 per month. You can choose from a variety of templates to create attractive emails, but the greater value of these services is in the data they provide. Just for starters, you'll know how many people opened your emails and on what devices, what links they clicked, and whether they shared with friends by forwarding or posting to social media.

Other typical features of email services include:

- CAN-SPAM compliance

- "Double opt-in" to confirm sign-ups. When people sign up, they get an email to verify that they really want to join your list. That prevents them from signing up others who might not be interested in your organization.

- List management to weed out defunct email addresses

- Optimized pages for mobile devices

- Segmentation, so you can email a subset of your subscribers based on where they live, for example, or what they're most interested in, or their level of engagement.

For do-it-yourself newsletter producers, several websites offer free boiler-plate email templates that are designed to display properly in Gmail, Yahoo! Mail, Outlook, and other major email clients. Here are two to try:

- HTML Email Boilerplate, http://htmlemailboilerplate.com

- Emailology, www.emailology.org

Another service, Email on Acid at www.emailonacid.com, allows you to see how your email will look in 48 variations of the most popular email clients. You can preview in AOL Mail, Outlook 2003, and Gmail for free. The full service is available in pay-as-you-go bundles or by monthly membership.

Start with a Calendar

Dennis McCarthy, coauthor of the Convio benchmarking report, says nonprofit leaders frequently ask him how often they should email their constituents. There's really no set answer, but most people are accustomed to getting email more frequently than direct mail.

NOTE: Monthly emailing is the most popular frequency for nonprofits, at 43 percent, followed by every other week at 19 percent, and quarterly at 14 percent, according to the *2012 Nonprofit Communications Trends Report*.

If you have good content to share, every month or six weeks is a reasonable interval. If there's an urgent need, say for fuel oil in an unusually cold winter, you can always reach out more often. That's another benefit of email, by the way: the ability to communicate on short notice.

Emails don't have to be—in fact, shouldn't be—only about donations. You can use them to deepen your connections with supporters by occasionally just sending photos or a short video of your group at work at, say, a food pantry or Habitat for Humanity build, or a beach cleanup.

If emailing every month to six weeks seems too frequent for you, a seasonal email schedule can work just as well. McCarthy suggests that small organizations draft a simple communications calendar to use as a framework for tasks and themes. For example:

- Spring is a time of rebirth. Send an email about a new program, or someone who has renewed hope because of your supporters. Make note of who's responsible for writing it.

- A summer email might be for a clothing drive or back-to-school effort.

- Thanksgiving is the perfect time to—yes—*thank* your supporters, letting them know that, for example, "to date, this is what we've accomplished with your support."

- In December, outline your plans for the coming year, and ask for an end-of-year donation.

NOTE: Small nonprofits are experiencing the fastest growth in online giving. Those with 10,000 or fewer email addresses grew median revenue by 26.7 percent in 2011. Those with email lists of 250,000 or more grew at only half that rate. Source: *The Convio Online Marketing Nonprofit Benchmark Index™ Study*.

As your capacity grows, consider adding an email or two each year written by someone who's received your services (but avoid solicitation). Also, have your executive director or president write once or twice a year, as the "voice" of your organization.

Write from the Heart

Now here's the potentially intimidating part: The writing. You can have great ideas for making the world a better place but still find yourself staring at a blank Word document. But guess what? You don't have to be a great writer, and you don't have to hire one, either.

Just write from your heart about what you do well. Definitely find someone to edit for spelling and grammar—you don't want outright errors. But your content doesn't have to be so polished that it sounds like it came from a magazine. In fact, some of the best emails are those where an executive director or a recipient of services writes a letter about your organization's impact. A real, heartfelt story lets people know that they're giving to a group that's making a difference.

The "real" image can be an advantage for small nonprofits. According to McCarthy's benchmark study, donations to large nonprofits are essentially flat year over year, while small organizations, food banks, and schools are continuing to see double-digit growth. People want to give locally, and they like to help fulfill the basic needs of others in their community.

Here are a few more best practices for email campaigns (**Figure 7.2**):

1. Feature a story about one relatable person who succeeded because of donors' generosity. (See our "storytelling" tips in Chapter 4.)

2. Include a small photo, but use mostly text. Not all of your readers can see images in email.

3. Write short, easy-to-read paragraphs. Use headings, bullets, and numbered lists to break up text and make it scannable.

4. Provide a clear call to action: Donate, register, volunteer, sign a petition, call your elected officials.

5. Offer information on how to contribute other than by donating.

6. Include a link for forwarding to a friend.

7. Provide an unsubscribe link.

8. Include your organization's address and phone number.

9. Write a short, punchy subject line. Shoot for 50 characters or less. (Many nonprofits ignore this.)

10. Use a recognizable "From" line, usually your organization's name.

11. Put key information at the top so it displays in email preview panes.

Figure 7.2 *This newsletter illustrates some of the best practices of email campaigns.*

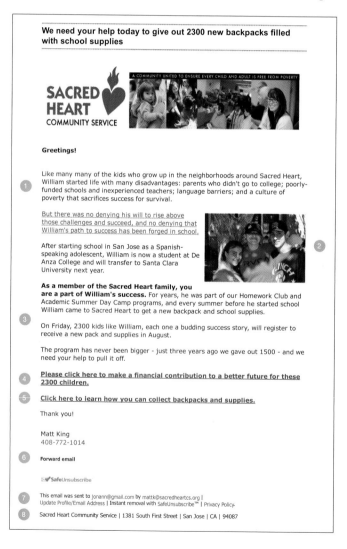

Multiple Channels, Multiple Gifts

In the past few years, large nonprofits in particular have paid close attention to multichannel giving, looking for insight into the habits and differences between online and offline donors.

Target Analytics, a Blackbaud company, conducts extensive research on the subject, looking into donor acquisition and retention, how much online and offline donors give over time, demographic differences, and more.

In the *2011 donorCentrics™ Internet and Multichannel Giving Benchmarking Report*, Blackbaud found that donors who were acquired online but gave offline as well gave three times more over five years than donors acquired by mail.

Other key findings about donors acquired online included the following:

- They tend to be significantly younger and have higher household incomes than donors acquired by mail.

- They tend to give larger gifts than mail-acquired donors.

- Their retention rates are slightly lower than those of mail-acquired donors.

The message that has emerged is that online and offline fundraising go hand in hand, and that nonprofits should have a presence everywhere their constituents are—from the telephone and the mailbox to Facebook and Twitter as well as Google Plus, Pinterest, YouTube, and Tumblr.

Good news, again! While all of that makes strategic sense for organizations that target prospects by the thousands, a small nonprofit can get by with a few well-chosen actions.

When you think of direct mail, you probably picture solicitation letters or print newsletters. But one of the most meaningful ways to use direct mail is the traditional handwritten thank-you note.

A personal thank-you stands in stark contrast to the speed and efficiency that online giving represents. It takes time and thought to compose, and that alone conveys your gratitude more genuinely than even the most sincere email could.

Convio's McCarthy, who recommends the communications calendar, likes the idea of designating a day or two a week for volunteers to write thank-you notes, perhaps on monarch-size paper for a distinguishing touch. Build that into your calendar so it becomes a habit.

Another good use of direct mail is to let your supporters know about events. An oversize postcard is perfect. The recipient can see what it's about right away, so the postcard is more likely to be read than a letter. And because there's no envelope, you can save a bit on postage.

In the spirit of multichannel integration, use your mailings to drive traffic to your website. It can be subtle on your thank-you notes—including your web address on your stationery—or more prominent on event postcards. There, you can direct readers to register or buy tickets online, "Like" the event on Facebook, or tweet about it.

Helping Hand

In terms of importance, email is second only to your website in your online fundraising efforts. A well-done email program will not only boost your budget, it will also help you stay connected and build an ongoing relationship with your constituents.

Here are some pointers to keep in mind:

- Your email list is a valuable asset. Make a concerted effort to build it.

- You can produce an e-newsletter yourself or use an email service provider. What matters most is heartfelt content that connects with supporters and shows them that they are having an impact.

- Event postcards and handwritten thank-you notes are easy and meaningful ways to use direct mail. Be sure to include your web address on your stationery to encourage visits to your website.

Next up in Chapter 8, we'll discuss apps, text-to-give, and other variations on mobile fundraising.

8

Going Mobile

Possibly the only gadgets we Americans love more than our tablet computers are our mobile phones, from which we can surf the Internet, play games, text, email, and even make actual phone calls occasionally.

The power of mobile fundraising became clear after the earthquake in Haiti in January 2010, when a Red Cross text-to-give campaign raised $43 million.

But here's that familiar pattern: While text-to-give and phone apps are the best-known methods of mobile fundraising, they're not the best starting points for small nonprofits. Let's look at some realistic options for the beginners.

The Unstoppable Smartphone

Cell phones have been commonplace for years now, so why all of a sudden is mobile such a buzzworthy topic? The answer is as close as your pocket or your purse: It's because of the exploding popularity of smartphones and their many capabilities.

Consider these statistics:

- As of June 2012, 54.9 percent of U.S. mobile subscribers owned smartphones, according to research by the Nielsen Company. In the third quarter of 2010, that number was only 28 percent.

- More than 90 percent of mobile users keep their phone no more than three feet away from them, 24 hours a day, seven days a week. (Yes, that includes the bathroom, and would probably include the shower if it wouldn't void the warranty.)

- Gartner research predicts that mobile phones will overtake personal computers as the most common Web-access devices worldwide by 2013. That milestone has already been reached in China, home of the world's largest online population. The Chinese government reported in July 2012 that 388 million people there used mobile phones in the first half of the year, while 380 million used computers.

- There are more iPhones sold worldwide each day than there are babies born.

Those numbers are dramatic indeed, and they make a strong case that nonprofits need a mobile strategy so they can reach supporters where they're most reachable.

Mobile is even more important when you're trying to reach a young audience. Teens and young adults will text until their thumbs go numb, but seldom check their (hopelessly old-school) email (**Figure 8.1**). So your time-sensitive alert or carefully crafted e-newsletter might very well go unseen by the youngest demographic.

One further consideration for charities that work with lower-income clients: Mobile access isn't always a matter of preference. For people who don't have a home computer, mobile phones might be their only way to access the Internet. It's doubly important for you to have a mobile-friendly website if you want to reach them.

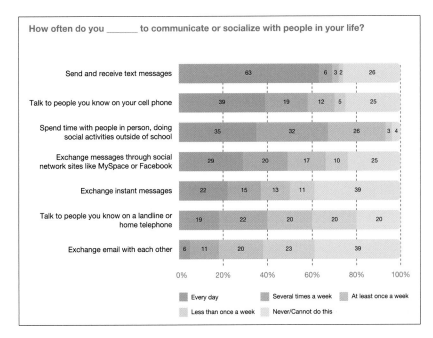

Figure 8.1

Sixty-three percent of teens say they exchange text messages every day. This far surpasses other forms of daily communication. Only 6 percent said they use email every day.

Source: Pew Internet & American Life Project, "Teens, Smartphones & Texting," March 19, 2012

Consider Your Priorities

We'll go over the various flavors of mobile fundraising and offer some ideas on how to incorporate them into your charity's plan. First, though, consider a slightly different perspective: for some organizations, the best use of mobile technology might not be for fundraising at all—at least not at first—but rather to enhance existing programs and increase engagement with supporters.

Larry Eason is the founder of DotOrgPower, which helps nonprofits use online and mobile technology to meet their goals. He suggests taking a step back and thinking about your organization's core priorities and initiatives and how mobile might fit in.

The resulting action could be as basic as improving communication with your supporters by providing them with information when and where they need it—texting volunteers if your tree-planting day is rained out, for example, or mobilizing them for an impromptu rally.

Another idea is to use mobile devices to build relationships: For one-on-one meetings with major donors, tell the story of your organization with a presentation on an iPad—an experience Eason says has been a success with his clients.

Presenting on a laptop is akin to putting a wall between you and your donor, he says, but sitting side by side flipping through a presentation together is an intimate and effective way to showcase your impact.

Nice-to-Haves

As a guideline, online strategists recommend starting to plan your mobile presence when 5 percent or more of your website traffic comes from mobile devices.

Once you hit that level and start investigating your options, you'll find that, yes, the choices are dizzying. And as we said earlier, the most familiar methods of mobile fundraising—text-to-give and apps—aren't very practical for the vast majority of small nonprofits.

Think of it this way: Your website and your email communication are your top online priorities. Next up (or better yet, concurrently) is making sure that your e-newsletter and at least a few key pages on your website are mobile friendly.

Most of the fundraising or community-building possibilities listed here are nice-to-haves for charities that have the budget or staff—or maybe a tech-savvy volunteer—to devote to them.

A mobile-friendly site, however, is firmly in the must-have category.

Remember back in Chapter 5 when we said that "if you build it, they will come" doesn't hold true for online fundraising—meaning that you can't slap a Donate button on your page and expect miracles?

Well, the mobile Web is altogether different—it *is* a classic example of "if you build it, they will come." In fact, a fair number of your supporters have been there for awhile, viewing your website from any number of mobile devices.

If you want them to keep coming back (and you do), then they have to be able to read and navigate your pages easily, whether they're viewing on a widescreen monitor at work, a tablet computer or e-reader on the sofa, or a 3.5-inch phone screen when they're crossing the street, listening to music, and eating a sandwich simultaneously.

Text-to-Give

With text-to-give, donors pledge $5 or $10 by texting a keyword ("HAITI," for example, **Figure 8.2**) to a special number called a short code. The pledged amount is added to the donor's phone bill.

Although hundreds of thousands of people gave $43 million to the Red Cross after the Haiti earthquake in January 2010, text-to-give isn't feasible for small nonprofits.

For starters, organizations have to report annual gross revenues of at least $500,000 to qualify. Also, it takes massive exposure—like appeals from the president on national television—to generate the kind of outpouring we saw for Haiti, and later, for victims of the 2011 earthquake and tsunami in Japan.

Even nonprofits that do qualify face some drawbacks with text-to-give. They don't collect valuable donor information that leads to ongoing relationships, because transactions are processed by the phone carrier, not the charity.

And because donations are limited to $5 or $10, nonprofits are essentially leaving money on the table, because many donors would give more if they could.

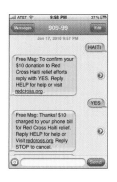

Figure 8.2 *The Red Cross text-to-give campaign raised $43 million for Haiti earthquake victims.*

Credit: Raffi Asdourian

Mobile Apps

Smartphone and tablet apps are mobile applications developed for specific device operating systems, such as Google's Android, Apple's iOS, BlackBerry, and Windows Mobile.

Apps offer the most polished user experience on mobile devices, but it can cost $15,000 to $50,000 to develop a custom app. Add in the costs of updating and maintaining an app in the various app stores, and the upside for a small charity dwindles rapidly.

Unless an app really adds a unique value, it seems most visitors would rather visit your website anyway. In a 2012 survey of more than 6,500 people ages 20–35 by the Millennial Impact project, 65 percent of respondents said their preferred way to find out about a nonprofit is through its website (**Figure 8.3**). In most cases, they said, the information in an app can be presented on a website just as easily.

Figure 8.3 *When Millennials want to learn about a nonprofit, most visit the organization's website first.*

Credit: *2012 Millennial Impact Report,* by Achieve and Johnson, Grossnickle and Associates

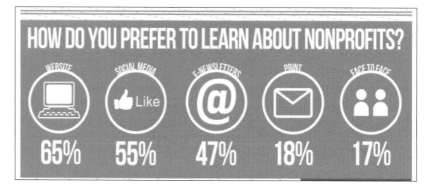

Of course, there are nonprofits whose missions naturally lend themselves to apps, some of which are accessible even without an Internet connection. Here are two notable examples:

● With the Monterey Bay Aquarium's Seafood Watch app (**Figure 8.4**), diners or shoppers can search to see which fish choices come from sustainable sources, and add to a map when they come across ocean-friendly stores and restaurants.

Figure 8.4 *The Seafood Watch app lets users sort seafood by "Best Choice," "Good Alternative," or "Avoid" rankings.*

Credit: © Monterey Bay Aquarium

- An app from the American Red Cross (**Figure 8.5**) gives step-by-step first aid information and lifesaving tips for emergencies. It also includes quizzes, videos, and checklists for emergency preparedness.

Figure 8.5
One feature in the American Red Cross First Aid app shows steps to take during an emergency, and includes a 9-1-1 call button.

If you still want to forge ahead and build an app for your charity, there's a good selection of free or low-cost app creators online if you have a modest budget and some technical ability:

- AppMakr, at www.appmakr.com, lets you compile text, audio, images, and video from around the Internet.

- Appafolio, at www.appafolio.com, is for creating portfolios and videos for iPad, iPhone, Android, and Kindle Fire.

- TAP, at www.tapintomuseums.org, allows museums to create mobile walking tours.

QR Codes

Quick Response codes, or QR codes, are those black-and-white boxes that look like Rorschach tests for robots (**Figure 8.6**). Like their bar code cousins, they can be attached to anything and everything (even escape-artist children).

When you scan a code with a reader app on your phone, you might be directed to a webpage or featured microsite, a video, a coupon, or other information (like the phone number for the escape artist's parents).

You can create codes for your organization for free (search the Web for QR code generators, there are many) and use them on posters, direct mail pieces, business cards—anything you like.

You can use them to send visitors to your website's Donate page, events calendar, or registration page, a petition, or anywhere else you want to direct their attention.

Wherever you send them, be sure it's to a page that's optimized for mobile devices (more on that in a minute) so it displays properly on a phone-sized screen. And be sure the content is compelling. If someone takes the time to scan a code, they're expecting something a little out of the ordinary.

Figure 8.6 *The Wikipedian in Residence at the Children's Museum of Indianapolis scans the QRpedia label within the exhibit,* National Geographic Treasures of the Earth. *The exhibit uses a QR code to direct users to the Wikipedia article "Captain Kidd's Cannon."*

Credit: cc-by-sa 2.0 by The Children's Museum of Indianapolis

Mobile Pledging

Mobile pledging, or text-to-pledge, is similar to text-to-give in that donors text a keyword to a short code. But this method doesn't involve phone carriers, so pledges aren't added to donors' mobile phone bills, and there isn't a $10 limit on donations.

Instead, the charity can receive donors' contact information and follow up later—say, calling the next day to get a credit-card number—or the mobile fundraising provider can handle fulfillment as part of its service.

Text-to-pledge is gaining traction at fundraising galas and other live events. A charity might display a thermometer with a fundraising goal and text instructions on a giant screen. As people in the audience text their pledges, their names (if desired) and donation amounts show up on the screen in real time.

The International Medical Corps raised $55,000 more than its goal using mobile pledging at an awards night fundraiser in November 2011. The group challenged attendees to match a $25,000 gift it had received from Research in Motion. They achieved that total in less than 10 minutes.

Location-Based Tools

Mobile apps that encourage users to "check in" at locations provide another way to expand your mobile presence.

You can claim (or create) your organization's page on Yelp, Foursquare, Facebook Places, and Google Places, to name a few. Compose some tips or special offers, and they'll display to visitors when they check in or when they're nearby.

Some charities have fashioned their own loyalty programs around these so-called "geosocial" sites, offering small perks for repeat check-ins or for their "mayors" or "dukes and duchesses"—fans who check in the most over a period of time.

The Brooklyn Museum, for example, honors its mayor with free membership for a year. At the San Jose Museum of Art, visitors who check in get a free poster with any purchase at the gift shop.

One fundraising strategy based on location-based tools is for nonprofits to partner with businesses for mutual benefit. Starbucks donated $1 to the Global Fund for every Foursquare check-in over a 10-day period in June 2012.

Those are huge organizations, but small nonprofits can adapt the idea on a local scale by striking similar deals with their neighborhood merchants. You could recommend a local store or restaurant to your clients, and the businesses could donate a small amount to your charity for every resulting check-in.

Geosocial sites present an opportunity to engage with supporters and clients, too. If people write about your organization on a site, pay attention. You can respond to online reviews publicly or privately, stay up to date about what's on your constituents' minds, and get a two-way conversation going. You could get together with a few active participants offline, or offer them a tour of your facility.

SMS/Texting

Short Message Service, or SMS, is a fancier way of saying "texting." It's the most used data application in the world, and the most likely to capture someone's attention (remember, most people have their phones within three feet of them nearly all the time.)

Research shows that 85 percent of people read a text message within 15 minutes of receiving it, while only 15 percent open an unread email.

A study of six large nonprofits uncovered more dramatic trends. According to the *2010 Nonprofit Text Messaging Benchmarks* study by M+R Strategic Services and MobileActive:

- Mobile list growth was 49.5 percent annually.

- Annual churn rate—mobile numbers that no longer work—for text lists was 30.7 percent.

- The benchmark text message unsubscribe rate was 0.69 percent.

- The response rate for advocacy texts asking people to call elected officials was 4.7 percent—six times higher than call-in advocacy emails.

Those are some compelling reasons to adopt texting on at least a small scale. You could send out reminders about trainings and events, and stay in communication with volunteers at walkathons and races. That's a good way to test the best uses for texting, too: Try it out internally with your staff and your most loyal supporters before launching a full-scale marketing campaign.

To start gathering mobile numbers, add a field to the email sign-up form on your website, collect them in person, and include a text-to-join number on your brochures and other materials. It doesn't hurt to build your list of numbers even if you don't plan to use them right away.

Think about what types of texts you'll send, how often, and of course, who's going to write them. One or two texts a month is just about right. That's enough to keep supporters informed and interested without crossing into the irritating zone.

Interestingly, younger people, who are the most avid texters in general, told the Millennial Impact project researchers that they text for personal reasons only. They don't want nonprofits to contact them by text or by phone.

As for the logistics of setting up group texting, you can select a vendor to set up your lists and manage the service, or you can look into a number of free options such as GroupMe, Kik Messenger, and textPlus.

Mobile Web

Ding! Ding! We have a winner! As you can see, there are oodles of opportunities to use mobile technology to engage with your constituents and fundraise for your cause. The ones mentioned above absolutely can enhance and extend your organization's reach (and some are just plain fun), but there's only one mobile offering that rises to the "essential" level: your mobile website.

That might seem like an added burden—you already have plenty to do to maintain your website and email communication, and now we're saying to design for people who don't look up from their phones long enough to cross the street.

But you do need to do it. There are easy(ish) ways to tackle it, and your supporters will have a much better experience because of it.

If your pages and emails don't look good or work properly on mobile phones, tablet computers, and e-readers, potential supporters might abandon your website and not come back.

For example, a nationally known hospital and a large chain restaurant added a QR code to their annual joint fundraising campaign in 2011, and the response was impressive. More than 290,000 people scanned the codes and landed on a simple, colorful page that offered three ways to participate.

So far so good!

The problem came in when kindhearted diners tapped the Donate button. The donation landing page had about a dozen fields to fill out, including credit-card numbers and required fields for address and phone number.

No doubt the page looked and functioned just fine on a desktop or laptop computer. But mobile friendly? Nope. The design overlooked the fact that diners would be coming to the Donate page from their phones. Keep in mind, these are users who shorten "you" to "u" to save keystrokes, so you (u?) can be sure that many potential donors dropped off rather than thumb-type 16-digit account numbers.

The lesson in that example is this: If the restaurant and hospital had optimized just one more page—the donation page—for mobile users, then their QR code campaign would've been not just impressive, but a total triumph.

Hold that thought, because it's an important one, especially if you're on a tight budget. You don't have to redesign your entire website to make sure it reads well on mobile devices.

TIP: Wondering how your website looks on various mobile phones or other devices? It's easy to find out. Do a Web search on "mobile device emulators," and you can preview your site on a variety of devices and browsers.

LOOKING GOOD ON THE SMALL SCREEN

There are several approaches to the mobile Web that make sense for small nonprofits. At minimum, you can optimize a few key pages. Websites built on open-source platforms can use plug-ins fairly easily to ensure mobile compatibility. Some organizations build a separate mobile site altogether.

- **Optimized pages.** If you aren't redesigning your website anytime soon, optimize the pages your mobile visitors go to the most: your homepage and donation page for sure, and maybe your email sign-up and events pages.

  These are some characteristics of mobile-friendly pages:

  – Simple layout, with no frames, tables, or pop-ups

  – Few graphics, small in size, to improve load time

  – No Flash video or JavaScript, which aren't supported on many mobile devices

  – "Tap to call" buttons or highlighted phone numbers to reduce typing

  – Minimal form fields to fill out. Get basic contact information, and follow up by phone if you need more.

  If your website already follows HTML best practices and isn't overly busy, it will probably look fine on most mobile browsers.

TIP: When your email newsletter links to a page on your website, be sure that landing page is mobile optimized. Your e-newsletter itself has to be readable on mobile devices, too. If it's not, you've probably wasted an email opportunity.

- **Update your current website.** Open-source platforms such as Word-Press, Drupal, Plone, and Joomla are widely used among nonprofits because they're free and customizable, and they make it comparatively easy to build and maintain a website.

  They also have plug-ins that adapt your site for mobile users. The plug-ins detect mobile browsers and reformat the pages into a single column. In some cases, all you have to do is install the right plug-in and enable it.

- **Create a separate, mobile-specific website.** This would be a stripped-down, task-oriented version of your website, with a limited number of links and images.

  For a nonprofit, a mobile homepage might have a small image and a handful of buttons—for example, Donate, What We Do, Contact Us, Events, and Get Services—plus a link to the full website.

  Web usability guru Jakob Nielsen favors this approach, arguing that the needs of mobile and desktop users are too different to satisfy with one design. He recommends "two designs, two sites, and cross-linking to make it all work."

  A vocal contingent of designers disagrees, however, saying that maintaining separate sites is time-consuming and ripe for errors if the two versions get out of sync.

- **Build a site with "responsive design."** If you're building your website from scratch or undertaking a redesign, then responsive design could be the best solution of all (**Figure 8.7**).

  With responsive design, website layouts adjust to fit browser windows of any width. The full-size homepage you see on your desktop monitor might display as one narrow column on a mobile phone, a wide column on a vertical tablet screen, and two columns when you turn the tablet to landscape view.

  Responsive design eliminates the need for zooming and scrolling, so websites are easier for users to navigate.

Figure 8.7 *A website built with responsive design will automatically resize to fit the screen it's viewed on.*

Credit: © 2012 The Aspen Institute (www.aspeninstitute.org) Site developed by Forum One Communications (www.forumone.com)

Helping Hand

The proliferation of smartphones has sparked excitement and innovation in the nonprofit sector. There are so many ways to use mobile technology that it's good practice to take stock of how it can enhance your existing programs, and then branch out from there.

- At minimum, your emails and your website's top three or four pages should be easy to read and navigate on smartphones.

- Texting is a practical way to stay in touch with volunteers and supporters. Start small, perhaps by using texts to coordinate with your staff at an event, rather than jumping right in with a text marketing campaign.

- Text-to-give and mobile apps are beyond the scope of most nonprofits. Focusing on your mobile Web presence is far more likely to serve your constituents.

The other hot area of online fundraising is social media. We'll look at the opportunities there in Chapter 9.

9

Getting Social

Posting.

Tweeting.

Pinning.

Flickr-ing. YouTubing. Google Plus-ing.

The proliferation of social media websites is enough to set your head spinning. How can you keep up with all that social networking when, you know, you have a nonprofit to run?

The fact is, you can't. There are simply too many social websites for you to manage them all well.

More than ever, you'll want to weigh the benefits of social media websites against the time and effort it takes to maintain them.

Social Media Goes Mainstream

Nonprofits have done their fair share to contribute to the momentum that has catapulted Facebook, Twitter, and other social media websites to incredible prominence (if not world domination) in a matter of a few years.

Researchers Nonprofit Technology Network (NTEN), Common Knowledge, and Blackbaud survey nonprofits about their social media habits each year. In their *2012 Nonprofit Social Network Benchmark Report,* they reported that 98 percent of their 3,500 respondents are on Facebook, up from 89 percent in 2011 and 74 percent in 2009.

Likewise, almost three-quarters—72 percent—are on Twitter, up from 57 percent in 2011. LinkedIn adoption was third highest, at 44 percent, followed by Google Plus at 23 percent.

At the individual level, it's not just the young'uns on social media, either. A 2012 survey by the Pew Research Center found that 53 percent of Americans over 65 use the Internet, and 34 percent of those are on Facebook or other social media websites.

PROGRESS BENCHMARKS

 ## Benefits of Social Media

Don't miss out on the many advantages of social media by thinking of it only as a means to raise money. It can enhance your organization in numerous ways, both tangible and intangible. Here are a few:

- As you monitor the social Web, you'll hear what your supporters and others are saying about your organization.

- You can quickly mobilize a grassroots campaign when something unexpected happens.

- You'll build trust by welcoming and responding to feedback from supporters and others who are interested in your organization or cause.

- Regular communications, even brief tweets or posts, will make your organization seem more approachable and human.

- You'll broaden your reach when you encourage supporters to help you get your message out through their social networks.

With numbers like that, you'd expect nonprofits to be swimming in donations, wouldn't you? Well ... no. As the researchers tactfully phrase it, "Facebook fundraising success is still enjoyed by just a select few."

And when they say "select few," they're not kidding. Of those groups that fundraise on Facebook, for example, 30 percent raised $1,000 or less in 2011. Only 2 percent raised $10,000 to $25,000.

If you look only at the modest amount of money raised, you could conclude that Facebook and other social media websites aren't especially successful for nonprofits. But don't let the words "why bother" pass your lips! Donations are only part of the value of social websites, and to look solely at that would be to miss the big picture. In Facebook parlance, "It's complicated."

The Network Effect

If you remember the '80s, you may remember the commercial in which a glossy-haired Heather Locklear's face multiplies exponentially across the TV screen because she tried a great shampoo and told two friends about it, "then they told two friends, and they told two friends, and so on, and so on, and so on!"

That is the beauty of social media. No, not the Heather Locklear part, the exponential growth part. If word gets around about your cause through social media, it's very likely that new visitors will check out your website, and possibly even donate or sign up for an event there.

So even though such a donation or action doesn't happen directly on Facebook or another social site, you still reap another benefit of social media: the ability to acquire new supporters at very low cost. That's a terrific benefit, but not one that's going to be captured in an analysis of dollars raised.

Pat Walsh, cofounder of social-fundraising solution StayClassy, considers the social Web more successful than traditional channels in some ways, because it promotes awareness and allows organizations to harness the energy of their most passionate supporters.

"The difference with social media is that it introduces personal connections and allows for back-and-forth discussion," Walsh says. "From a causes perspective in particular, that personal connection makes a huge difference. Someone in my network is sharing their support for this particular cause, and as a result, I'm more inclined to support it myself."

So with that, let's get a quick overview of the social Web.

Social Media Heavyweights

The ascension of sites like Facebook, YouTube, Twitter, and Flickr has brought us true social media: a huge, always-on conversation using text and multimedia that anyone can watch and join.

All of these social media sites, and others, are more than just fun ways to share your life with friends and family (though they're good at that, too). Social sites provide an incredible outlet for your organization to reach current and future supporters, and they each do it in their own way.

 Facebook is a robust and open platform for nonprofits and businesses. One of its key features is Pages, which are essentially profiles for organizations instead of individuals.

Pages basically function as self-contained blogs within the larger Facebook framework. But they have some much cooler features, such as the capability to add fundraising applications (FundRazr, Causes) and events pages, which in turn can expand the experience for your page's visitors.

Add photos, thank donors and volunteers, set up quizzes and polls; there are innumerable ways to engage with your community on Facebook.

 The idea behind microblogging website **Twitter**'s creation was simple: to enable phone text messages to be shared and displayed on the Web. Because of texting's 140-character limit, the same limitation was applied to Twitter messages, or "tweets."

Tweets are read mostly by a Twitter user's followers, though the general public can view them too.

Tweets often include hashtags (#), which enable them to be organized around specific news, people, issues, or events. For example, a Twitter user can see what's on the minds of nonprofit leaders by setting up a filter to view all messages tagged with #nonprofits. Be sure to follow your own and similar organizations' names to see what topics are top of mind at a given time.

Your own tweets can be a mix of commentary, calls to action, event information, pitches for fundraising drives, and shout-outs to volunteers or donors. Experiment a little and see what types of tweets generate the most response from your particular audience.

Pinterest is the up-and-comer of social media, exploding in popularity in 2012. Users "pin" online images to virtual "pinboards"—not unlike scrapbooking, really—to express their interests or save ideas for decorating, fashion, cooking, or anything else.

Because it's so new, nonprofits are still finding their way toward the best uses of Pinterest. Infographics are gaining traction with some charities to boost advocacy. Others feature photos from their events, or inject some whimsy—as in the #Squirrels4Good gallery by the National Wildlife Federation at http://pinterest.com/nwfpins/squirrels4good/.

Pinterest's demographic is overwhelmingly female. If your cause is of special interest to women, it could be a good spot to build your audience.

LinkedIn is a social network for professionals and a good place to communicate with your nonprofit peers. By using connections and joining groups within LinkedIn, you can reach out to fellow organizations to get direct information and share ideas.

Quora is an online question-and-answer hub. Quora users ask questions about any particular topic, which are then answered by other users. Answers are often written by authorities in their fields. It's not unusual for a question about a nonprofit to be answered by an executive in that organization.

Those are just some of the players in social media. If you want to explore further, check out Flickr, Instagram, YouTube, Tumblr, and Google Plus.

10 Steps to Success

1. Set Your Strategy

Before you get started, think about your goals for social media, and coordinate them with your other marketing methods. Is raising awareness your priority? Building your email list? Deepening engagement? You probably want to do all of those things, but solidifying your goals will keep you focused.

TIP: Just as with your email newsletters, maintain a calendar to plan your social media activities and sync them with your other events and communications. Experiment with various types of content, and mix it up: for example, share your news in one blog post or tweet, present a call to action in the next, and then post a poll.

It's important to recognize that like most technology, tools will change, and often very quickly. Many social media networks could be all but obsolete in a year or less. That's the nature of technology.

This is why it's critical to craft your organization's message, and then push that message out on the platforms where your supporters are.

Finding the right social media platform is especially important for small organizations that don't have a lot of staff resources to devote to multiple websites. Instead of trying to be everywhere, pick the one or two websites that reach your biggest audience, and concentrate on updating them regularly.

On less-visited social sites, list your organization's basic information and refer visitors to your homepage and your Facebook page, for example, for further updates.

TIP: Even if your organization is small and informal, you probably want to talk to your board members and staffers about your foray into social media. A few discussions about how you'll handle any problems that could arise, and what is and isn't OK to share, can head off some unpleasant surprises.

2. Allocate Your Resources

Just because tweets are short and sweet doesn't mean just anyone should toss them off. It also doesn't mean it's a 10-minute task. Updating your social media will require time and commitment.

In the *Social Network Benchmark Report* referenced above, researchers said successful nonprofits were in "unambiguous, broad agreement" that three factors were key to doing well in social media:

1. They developed a strategy.

2. Their executive team supported their efforts.

3. They had a dedicated staff, even if social media was only a portion of their job.

Decide who will handle your social media updates, and how long to spend on them each day or couple of days. If more than one person is involved, think about division of labor: maybe one person updates Facebook, while another blogs, or maybe everyone works on every platform.

Keep in mind that writing and posting isn't the only task. It takes time to find and respond to comments, look through alerts, and vet user-generated content, too.

3. Research Your Audience

If you're not really sure where your supporters hang out online—and therefore, where you should too—just ask them!

It's almost a given that your organization should be on Facebook, and that supporters and casual visitors alike would expect to find you there. Twitter is probably the next best-known social media platform, but it's not necessarily where your audience is. Those hashtags and at signs (@) are just confusing enough to scare some people away.

If you're an arts organization or other group with inherent visual appeal, or if your supporters are largely female, then you might want more of a presence on Pinterest or Flickr.

If you want to connect with potential supporters or build your reputation as a thought leader, then weighing in on LinkedIn Groups or answering questions on Quora could be the way to go.

You can ask your constituents about their social media habits through your email newsletters, at events, or when they visit your office. Another approach is to conduct a simple online survey (see sidebar).

Be proactive, too. Let people know that you are on the Internet, and encourage them to follow you.

4. Join Conversations

At first, you might be tempted to simply tell the social media universe about the awesomeness of your organization. There's certainly no harm in highlighting your staff and your achievements, but complement that by featuring donors, volunteers, and clients who are likely to inspire comments.

Remember, conversation is what puts the "social" in "social media." Just as you want to engage visitors on your website—not just barrage them with information that's all about you—be prepared to engage them on social sites. When you do, you'll tap into the main value of social media: the ability to hold a conversation with someone, while everyone else can listen and chime in, too.

Industry INSIDER ————————————————————————

 Online Survey Tools

Online surveys are a quick and easy way to gather information about your supporters' habits and preferences. Even better, there are many online tools that are available for free or at low cost for simple questionnaires. Here are a few that non-profits typically use:

- **SurveyMonkey**, www.surveymonkey.com. Free version offers 10 questions and 100 responses per survey. You can collect data via weblink, email, or Facebook, or embed questions on your site or blog.

- **Google Forms**, www.google.com/google-d-s/forms/. Questions can be shared from links, emailed, or embedded in a website. Responses are organized in a Google spreadsheet.

- **Polldaddy**, www.polldaddy.com. Free version permits 10 questions per survey and 200 responses per month. Basic reports for polls, surveys, quizzes.

- **FluidSurveys**, www.fluidsurveys.com. Free plan features unlimited surveys, with up to 20 questions and 150 responses per survey.

Strike a balance between talking and listening. People will mostly want to learn from you about your cause and the issues in your field, but they'll expect to be heard when they do have something to tell you.

Conversations aren't limited to your own websites, either. As your time allows, visit top blogs and websites in your field and comment when appropriate. As mentioned above, answering questions on LinkedIn Groups or Quora not only helps the asker, but also over time positions you as an influencer. And of course there's the obvious benefit of rubbing virtual elbows with potential new supporters in those groups.

5. Find the Right Tools

If you're active on more than one social media platform, you'll want to consider some tools to help you track your own organization's activity, and to stay up to date on people and topics that are relevant to your cause.

TweetDeck and HootSuite, for example, let you schedule tweets or posts, and track how many mentions or retweets you get. Scheduling ahead of time is especially handy if you don't have time to update every day, but don't want all of your posts or tweets to come out at once.

Social Mention monitors more than 100 social media websites and sends you alerts on the organizations, individuals, or issues you choose. Facebook Insights provides information on how visitors interact with your Facebook page.

Set up Google Alerts for your organization's name and the names of thought leaders and other organizations in your field so you can keep abreast of news and trends.

TIP: Need ideas for what to blog or tweet or post about? Use the same approach as for your website: highlight a coming event, profile a staffer/donor/volunteer, thank someone for a notable gesture, post photos, or preview your next newsletter.

6. Give the People What They Want

One great way to figure out the most relevant content is to determine what your visitors want when they come to your organization's website, blog, or social media site.

As users look for information about your organization or your cause, they'll plug search terms—say, food banks or women's shelters—into their favorite search engine. If your content is a match, your site will be prominently displayed in the search results.

TIP: Google Grants is a program that awards qualifying nonprofits $10,000 per month in advertising on Google through AdWords. Go to www.google.com/grants/ for details.

These organic searches will help you figure out what content is most interesting to your visitors, and what will likely be interesting to them in the future. This is search engine optimization 101: tailoring your content to attract the attention of the audience and customers you want. Using these kinds of SEO analytics can be of great assistance in creating your social media conversations.

Most analytics tools, such as the free-of-charge Google Analytics, can provide insight into what's bringing your visitors to your website. By tapping into these tools, such as the Matched Search Queries page, you can see what search terms people are using to find you.

If people are coming to your site looking for information about a particular topic, then you can start framing social media conversations around that topic and related ones.

7. Use Rich Media

Producing compelling content is great—essential, really—but what if you could go further and inspire users to contribute content of their own?

There are several ways to encourage users to contribute to your social media channels. One is through rich multimedia content, which these days is as easy to produce as pulling out your cell phone.

Use polls, images, and video to get your audience involved in the conversation. You could post photos or video from your fundraising auction to Flickr or Instagram and YouTube, and invite attendees to do the same.

Theater groups could record snippets of performers rehearsing for behind-the-scenes videos. Or try a simple tour of your facility to build familiarity with your audience.

8. Listen to Your Audience

Once you have a good idea of where your supporters spend their time online, see what they're saying. What's the hot topic in your field right now? Is it related to a service you provide? How is the tone of the discussion?

These are concepts that you will need to note as you listen to the conversation. Hold off on responding for a bit; wait a few days to get the gist of the discussion.

For instance, are your peers in the conversation? What are they saying? You don't want to parrot them, because you'll sound like someone who's just a "me too" sort of chatterer. Listen to what's being said and by whom. You may find yourself agreeing or disagreeing with a lot of ideas, so you'll want to take the time to figure out what you're going to say and to whom.

Another use of social media channels is to utilize them as a direct conduit to your constituents. For small organizations, this is an ideal way for supporters and clients to get their questions asked and answered.

Even if you're active on only one or two social media sites, you'll still want to check in on others (say, Yelp and Foursquare) when you can to look for questions and reviews. Respond as promptly and completely as possible to negative comments as well as positive.

9. Build Community

When building a community with social media, make it a point to put the community first. An online community can foster loyalty to your organization, build relationships among your supporters, and generate ideas to help you raise more money.

In the broader sense, engage with your community by retweeting Twitter updates from organizations similar to yours. Comment on others' blogs, and include a link to your website or social sites.

Conferences are a great source of the most current topics in any field. Share links to presentations, or even live-tweet sessions that you think your supporters would like to follow.

Invite your supporters to share their own photos or videos of events on your social pages. Ask a volunteer to guest-write a blog entry or Facebook update.

10. Measure Your Results

There are quite a few social media metrics that you can begin tracking right away. You can dig into them as deeply as you'd like, but for most organizations just starting in social media, it's fine to start small. Some of the basics:

- Number of Facebook "Likes"

- Number of tagged photos

- Number of email sign-ups or event registrations

- Number of Twitter followers

- Number of retweets or mentions

- Number of photos or videos viewed on Flickr or YouTube

Other valuable analytics to track include which social sites your visitors are coming from, what articles they're sharing and where, and which sites sent visitors who donated on your pages.

Helping Hand

As we've seen, there are numerous ways for nonprofits to approach social media, depending on their goals, staffing levels, and supporters' interests. Getting it right is likely to take some trial and error. These key suggestions will make life a little easier for small organizations:

- Concentrate on one or two social media websites so you can update them consistently without spreading yourself too thin.

- Use social media to engage in a conversation with your constituents. Listen and respond to them to increase loyalty.

- You'll benefit from that loyalty when your supporters are motivated to tell their friends about your mission. Most people are more likely to support a cause if they hear about it from a friend than if they're solicited in some other way.

Part 4

FUNDRAISING
WITH PAYPAL

10

How PayPal Works

If you've ever shopped online or bought and sold on eBay, you're probably familiar with PayPal. PayPal enables businesses and nonprofits of all sizes, as well as individuals, to accept bank or credit card payments online, via mobile devices, and in-store.

When one of your supporters buys your organization's wristband or T-shirt, or makes a donation through PayPal, PayPal processes the payment and transfers the funds to your PayPal account.

Read on to see how PayPal can help your organization raise more money and do more good.

Why Use PayPal?

PayPal offers benefits to both nonprofit organizations and their donors.

Nonprofits can tap into the PayPal account-holder base to acquire new donors.

It can also give regular donors a safer, more secure way to donate online 24/7 from anywhere PayPal is available.

When your nonprofit uses PayPal, donors don't have to share their financial information, and your organization can spend less time and money processing paper checks.

PayPal and Nonprofits

Ranjana Clark, PayPal's senior vice president, chief customer and marketing officer, says PayPal and parent company eBay Inc. "aspire to change the world through technology-led social innovation."

Both the eBay and PayPal platforms enable nonprofits to reach donors worldwide, and to raise the funds and the awareness they need to pursue their missions. In 2011, more than 200,000 charitable organizations received more than $3 billion through PayPal, and the eBay community raised an additional $63 million through eBay Inc. giving programs.

Behind the Scenes

We know PayPal's mission at a high level, but how does it work down on the ground (or at the computer)? **Figure 10.1** illustrates the payment process.

NOTE: PayPal is secure, so your supporters can donate knowing their financial information will be protected. Also, since payment takes place over PayPal's secure webpages, you don't have to worry about PCI compliance or storing customer data for PayPal transactions.

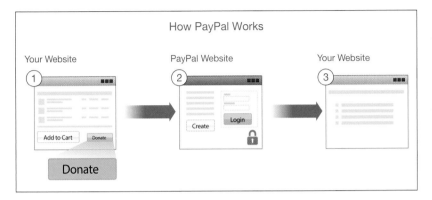

Figure 10.1

1. On your non-profit's website, donors click the Donate button.

2. Donors complete secure donations on PayPal's site using their preferred method of payment.

3. Donors return to your site, and your organization receives funds in your PayPal account quickly. Transfer these funds to your organization's checking account at no charge.

PayPal Mobile Express Checkout

We talked in Chapter 8 about how important it is to have a mobile-friendly website. PayPal took that leap in 2010 with the introduction of Mobile Express Checkout, which simplifies the checkout/donation process for people using mobile devices.

With Mobile Express Checkout, users of iPhones, iPads, Android devices, BlackBerrys, and Windows Phone 7 see optimized pages for smaller mobile screens and mobile keyboards.

Donors don't have to enter their billing address, email, phone number, and credit card information as they would in the typical checkout. All they enter is a password or PIN.

PayPal provides all of the required information to you, which allows the donor to skip all of the data-collection pages.

If you have already integrated Express Checkout on your website, you can add Mobile Express Checkout with minimal programming changes.

PayPal Here

Another new PayPal offering that nonprofits have embraced is PayPal Here, a credit card reader that plugs into smartphones for in-person sales and donations. (Imagine the convenience for everyone involved when silent auction winners pay by simply swiping their cards.) You can even scan checks with the camera on your phone.

PayPal Here is especially attractive when you consider that 90 percent of fundraising still happens at real-world events: silent auctions, runs and rides, galas, car washes, bake sales, and more. Until recently, nonprofits that wanted to accept anything other than cash or checks at those events had only limited, and expensive, options: high transaction fees plus equipment to rent (or buy), or the risks of writing down credit card numbers on paper to process back at the office later.

PayPal Here makes it safer, easier, and cheaper to collect funds in person, and it improves your cash flow because you know immediately how much you've raised from both online and offline efforts.

Fees for Nonprofits

PayPal offers discounted transaction fees for registered 501(c)(3) organizations.

Your organization must provide documentation of its 501(c)(3) status to receive the discounted transaction rates. To confirm your nonprofit's status, log in to your PayPal account one day after initial sign-up and submit the following items through the Resolution Center:

- Evidence of tax-exempt status

- Bank statement or voided check in your organization's name

- PayPal email account

- Contact information

- Description of your organization and type of payments you want to accept (such as donations and merchandise payments)

Discounted pricing will not apply to your account until you have received an email from PayPal verifying your nonprofit status.

The following rates apply for PayPal Payments Standard, Express Checkout, and PayPal Payments Pro:

- $100,000 or less in monthly volume: 2.2% + $.30 per domestic transaction. (Discounted rates do not apply to American Express transactions made using PayPal Payments Pro and Virtual Terminal.)

- More than $100,000 in monthly volume: call 866-365-6319 for rates.

Rates are subject to change, but are current as of October 2012.

If your organization does not have 501(c)(3) status, you'll pay our standard transaction rates. See www.paypal.com/fees for more information.

Managing Your Data

PayPal's Reporting Tools provide you with the information you need to effectively measure and manage your nonprofit. With PayPal's Reporting Tools, you can

- Analyze your revenue sources to better understand your donors' behavior.

- Automate time-consuming bookkeeping tasks.

- Accurately settle and reconcile transactions.

These are some of the tools that make it easier to track your finances. A side note: Because your nonprofit PayPal account is a Merchant account, your reports will refer to "sales," but that term applies to donations as well.

- **History Log:** View an online record of your payments received and sent.

- **Downloadable Logs:** Keep track of your transaction history by downloading it into various file formats (suitable for financial settlements).

- **Monthly Account Statements:** View and print up to three past months of transactions on your account. Each month's statement provides totals of payments received, fees, and other credits and debits for each day, so you can more easily track your transactions.

- **Transaction Finder:** Search for transactions by customer/donor name, business name, eBay user ID, and more. You can narrow your search by selecting options such as date range or transaction amount. With these search parameters you can find the exact information you want faster, enabling you to respond to your customers more efficiently.

Finding Out More

If you want to learn more about PayPal, visit the nonprofit section of the website at www.paypal.com/nonprofit. You'll find FAQs, video demos, information on PayPal Here, and more.

Individual fundraisers who aren't part of a nonprofit can find similar information at www.paypal.com/fundraise. Also on this page is a link for political fundraising for local, state, and national campaigns.

In addition, the PayPal website offers a Help Center that's reachable from a link on any page. You can browse a range of support topics, or search for the topic you need.

In PayPal's Community Help forum, users answer each other's questions. For visual learners, there's a link to a selection of short how-to videos on YouTube.

Helping Hand

- As one of the world's largest online payment services, PayPal provides credit card processing and other services for individuals, businesses, and nonprofits.

- Mobile Express Checkout lets nonprofits offer supporters a simplified checkout process, and PayPal Here allows for in-person payments.

- Registered 501(c)(3) nonprofits receive discounts on fees.

Conclusion

In conversations with nonprofit leaders, we've heard time and again how difficult it is for the smallest nonprofits to incorporate online fundraising into their strategies. Some organizations don't have anyone to maintain more than a bare-minimum website, while others would love to build out their sites but don't really know what to put on them.

We hope you come away from this book with at least a few simple, actionable ideas of what you can do online right away (say it with us... "Donate button"), and what you'll want to add in the future when the time is right (newsletters, text campaigns, social media).

Every charity has a story to tell, and you don't have to be slick to tell it well. If you convey with sincerity the emotional pull that attracted you to your cause in the first place, you'll be well on your way to bringing others along on your fundraising journey.

Thanks for reading, and thanks even more for making the world better for others.

Appendix

Reader Resources

The nonprofit universe has an incredibly rich presence on the Internet. You can find all the ideas and advice and how-tos you could ever need, for any and every cause you could ever imagine.

Following is just a sampling of some that you might find useful.

Industry Associations

Association of Fundraising Professionals (AFP), www.afpnet.org/
Professional association of individuals and organizations that generate
philanthropic support for a wide variety of charitable institutions

Nonprofit Technology Network (NTEN), www.nten.org/
Membership organization of nonprofit technology professionals

Trade Shows and Conferences

Blackbaud Conference for Nonprofits, www.bbconference.com/

Bridge to Integrated Marketing & Fundraising Conference,
www.bridgeconf.org/

Emerging Practitioners in Philanthropy, www.epip.org/

International Conference on Fundraising,
http://conference.afpnet.org/registration.cfm

National Conference on Volunteering and Service,
www.volunteeringandservice.org/2013-conference.cfm

Nonprofit Technology Conference, www.nten.org/ntc

Social Media for Nonprofits, http://socialmedia4nonprofits.org/

Washington Nonprofit Conference,
http://www.the-dma.org/conferences/

Young Nonprofit Professionals Network National Leaders Conference,
www.ynpnconference.org/

Blogs and Websites

501(c)(3) University, www.501c3.org/501c3-university/
Online source for nonprofit education

Beth's Blog, www.bethkanter.org/
One of the longest running and most popular blogs for nonprofits

Charity Navigator, www.charitynavigator.org/
Nation's largest independent charity evaluator

Crowdrise, www.crowdrise.com/
Online tools for personal fundraising, event fundraising, special occasion fundraising, team fundraising, and sponsored volunteerism

DonateNow, http://donatenow.com/
Portal for charities and donors

DotOrgPower, www.dotorgpower.com/
Helps nonprofit leaders plan and succeed online

FirstGiving, www.firstgiving.com/
Tools to manage online fundraising

FundRaising Success magazine, www.fundraisingsuccessmag.com/

FundRazr, https://fundrazr.com/
Personal fundraising with social media integration

Gail Perry, Fired-Up Fundraising, www.gailperry.com/

Givezooks! www.givezooks.com/
Social fundraising for nonprofits

GoFundMe, www.gofundme.com/
Create personal, business, group, or organization fundraising websites.

GoodSearch, www.goodsearch.com/
Search engine that donates 50 percent of its sponsored search revenue to the charities and schools designated by its users

Google Analytics, www.google.com/analytics/

Google Groups, https://groups.google.com/

Google Grants, www.google.com/grants/

GuideStar, www.guidestar.org/
Lists and evaluates thousands of public charities

HelpAttack! www.helpattack.com/
Social media users pledge a small amount to a charity each time they tweet, update their Facebook status, post on a blog, or take some other social action.

Indiegogo, www.indiegogo.com/
A crowdfunding platform where people who want to raise money can create fundraising campaigns to tell their story and get the word out

IRS Stay Exempt: Tax Basics for Exempt Organizations, www.stayexempt.org/

JustGive, www.justgive.org/
Helps individuals find charities to support

Katya's Non-Profit Marketing Blog, Katya Andresen, www.nonprofitmarketingblog.com/

Kivi's Nonprofit Communications Blog, Kivi Leroux Miller, www.nonprofitmarketingguide.com/blog/

National Association of Attorneys General, www.naag.org/

National Association of State Charity Officials, www.nasconet.org/

Network for Good Learning Center, www.fundraising123.org/

Sandy Rees, Get Fully Funded, http://getfullyfunded.com/

Socialbrite, www.socialbrite.org/
Helps nonprofits with social media

Unified Registration Statement, www.multistatefiling.org/

Yahoo Groups, http://groups.yahoo.com/

Books

Donor-Centered Fundraising,
by Penelope Burk (Cygnus Applied Research, Inc., 2003).

Invisible Ink: A Practical Guide to Building Stories that Resonate,
by Brian McDonald (Libertary, 2010).

The Networked Nonprofit: Connecting with Social Media to Drive Change,
by Beth Kanter and Allison H. Fine (Jossey-Bass, 2010).

Research and Surveys

2010 Nonprofit Text Messaging Benchmarks,
http://labs.mrss.com/2010-nonprofit-text-messaging-benchmarks-study/

2011 donorCentrics™ Internet and Multichannel Giving Benchmarking Report, www.blackbaud.com/targetananalytics/multi-channel-report

2012 Nonprofit Communications Trends Report,
www.nonprofitmarketingguide.com/resources/book/2012-nonprofit
-communications-trends-report/#

2012 Nonprofit Social Network Benchmark Report,
http://nonprofitsocialnetworksurvey.com/download.php

2011 Online Giving Report, Blackbaud,
www.blackbaud.com/onlinefundraising

Comparison of Email Service Providers 2012,
http://groundwire.org/labs/email-publishing/2012-email-service-providers

A Consumers Guide to Low Cost Donor Management Systems,
http://www.idealware.org/reports/consumers-guide-low-cost-donor
-management-systems

The Convio Online Marketing Nonprofit Benchmark Study,
https://content.blackbaud.com/BenchmarkReport.html

Giving USA Reports, www.givingusareports.org/

Homer Simpson for Nonprofits: The Truth about How People Really Think and What It Means for Promoting Your Cause,
http://web.networkforgood.org/201002ebook/

Idealware, www.idealware.org/
Idealware, a 501(c)(3) nonprofit, provides researched, impartial, and accessible resources about software to help nonprofits make smart software decisions.

Lisa Simpson for Nonprofits: What Science Can Teach You About Fundraising, Marketing and Making Social Change,
http://web.networkforgood.org/2011-03-ebook-lisa-simpson-ntc/

The Millennial Impact,
http://themillennialimpact.com/millennial-report/

The Next Generation of American Giving,
www.convio.com/signup/next-generation/next-generation-resources.html

Teens, Smartphones & Texting, Pew Internet & American Life Project,
http://pewinternet.org/Reports/2012/Teens-and-smartphones.aspx

Technical Tools

Appafolio, http://appafolio.com/

AppMakr, www.appmakr.com/

BBNow, http://bbnow.org/
Website builder integrated with PayPal

Drupal, http://drupal.org/
Open source content management platform powering millions
of websites and applications

Emailology, www.emailology.org/

Email on Acid, www.emailonacid.com/

FluidSurveys, http://fluidsurveys.com/

Google Forms, www.google.com/google-d-s/forms/

GroupMe, https://groupme.com/
Free group texting

HTML Email Boilerplate, http://htmlemailboilerplate.com/

Joomla, www.joomla.org/
Content management system for building websites and online
applications

Kik Messenger, http://kik.com/
Smartphone messenger

Plone, http://plone.org/
Open source content management

Polldaddy, http://polldaddy.com/

SurveyMonkey, www.surveymonkey.com/

TAP, http://tapintomuseums.org/

TextPlus, www.textplus.com/
Free group texting

WordPress, http://wordpress.org/
Open source content management

Index